ARCHIVES OF
A GHOST HUNTER II

CRAIG NEHRING AND MELISSA CLEVENGER

TABLE OF CONTENTS

ABOUT THE AUTHORS

Craig Nehring is well known in the Minocqua area where he graduated from Lakeland High School in 1988. He was an avid water skier on Plum-Skiters and Manitowish Waters Skiing Skeeters for fifteen years combined. There was no skill test that he took in school that said he would become a professional paranormal researcher.

Craig is the founder of Fox Valley Ghost Hunters and co author of Wisconsin's Most Haunted Vol 1 & 2. He is author of *Archives of a Ghost Hunter* released at the end of 2018. Craig has been featured on U.S. Cellular Commercials in 2016 and some of them have over 4 million views. He has been on radio shows from Coast to Coast, Late Night in the Midlands, Fade to Black, Hillbilly Podcast and on Beyond Reality with Jason Hawes (star of the Ghost Hunting show TAPS). Our team has been featured in newspapers from the *Huffington Post* to *Milwaukee Journal*. We have been in the biggest paranormal magazines out there called Paranormal Underground Magazine.

Craig's bucket list consists of the Bran Castle, Alcatraz, and more. The team will have numerous opportunities in 2020 and 2021 to be on the TV shows for various haunted locations around Wisconsin and other states.

Melissa Clevenger joined Fox Valley Ghost Hunters in March of 2018, and she is the lead investigator for the team. She has been on numerous radio shows, spoken at several events, and has devoted most of her time to investigating the unknown. The paranormal is a part of her life and a part of who she is.

Melissa was born in 1979 growing up in Marquette, a small farming community in central Kansas. Her experiences with the paranormal started at a very young age. She would always see ghosts and they would communicate with her.

Melissa now lives in Sheboygan, Wisconsin with her husband Travis and their three kids (Taylor 18, Kaleb 6, and Colton 4). She has traveled to countless notorious haunted locations checking off her bucket list. Delving into the history of the locations that she investigates intrigues her. Through the years her ability to see ghosts has faded, but her passion to communicate continues.

INTRODUCTION

In the last Archives of a Ghost Hunter we covered almost all out of state investigations. This time we take you on a journey of our investigations throughout the Midwest including Wisconsin. With so many haunted locations to choose from we bring you to some of the scariest places we could find. We take you inside these haunted locations and tell you firsthand our experiences and what we captured while investigating.

In this book the term Ghost and Spirit is used in the same content; however, in some beliefs the term Ghost is referred to someone still on earth and while the term Spirit is someone that has passed over to heaven or another realm and is able to come back at free will. A ghost can appear in a form and likes to haunt people and can sometimes be mischievous. A Spirit appears in a misty form otherwise known as an apparition and is not there to haunt someone but to watch over things.

Our investigations are real and never faked and all our evidence is legit. Following the numerous shows on TV one can find that things happen all the time. We spend many hours waiting for something to happen and sometimes nothing ever happens. Remember the TV shows must keep you entertained. Don't always believe what you see on TV. I would like to thank all our followers, friends, and family for the support over the years.

CHAPTER 1

NEW FRANKEN HOUSE

By Craig Nehring

We got a call in 2018 to come and investigate a house in New Franken, Wisconsin which was featured on a Dead Files episode on TV. We jumped at the idea to go to a place that was investigated by well-known TV stars. The owner called me and explained that since the show was on things were still happening and said they would have to move out soon but wanted to know if we would like to investigate and see what we find in caparison to the what the show had captured.

I decided to dig a little bit into the history of the house before our team goes to the location to see if we can pick up on some names or why the house could be haunted. I found that the house was built in 1856 and originally had 82 acres. In 1889, a gentlemen by the name of John Joseph Delvaux owned the property and had some problems involving a scandal which involved local politics involving a bribe. That same year his wife Mary of sixty-nine years passed away in the house. His son Joseph dies a short time later from turberculosis at the age of twenty-nine. In 1893 John dies of kidney failure at the age of sixty-nine the same age of his wife when she passed away. All these deaths were on the property and through the years three more deaths were reported with two of them from consumption. So with all these deaths on the property and all this sadness it may be possible they still inhabit the house even after death.

I watched the episode of Dead Files to get a feel for what they found. They said that the house had some bad vibes and since the owners remodeled for their business things got worse for them. Changing the surroundings caused things to stir up and get more violent. The investigators of the show stated that something was outback behind the house watching whoever lived in the house and was attached to the land. They also said there were dark figures roaming the house and they were not pleasant and wanted everyone to leave. It was their house and they wanted the humans gone. I called the owners to find out what they had encountered. The owner Lily said when they started to remodel the house and tear some walls down, they found old newspaper clipping in the walls. They also found clothing, boots, and a womens corset. Once all the stuff was out of the walls things began to happen. They would hear voices, see shadows moving about the house, and hear footsteps. When they would go to the basement they would hear footsteps upstairs and doors would slam. One time while in the basement she heard a loud growl come from a small room off the basement that was solid cement with no windows. Lily said she felt as though she was watched all the time while just doing normal things in the house. They wanted to have a business in their home and now they were giving up on it since things had gotten so bad for them. We set up a date for us to come out and investigate.

The Investigation of New Franken Home

We arrived on location with team members Celena, John, and Lloyd. We picked a very cold night and had to bring some heaters with us to place in a room to keep warm. Looking at the place from the outside made me think I could turn this house into a bowling alley. It was a long house with white siding that went on forever. The back of the house had a barn left over from many years ago and beyond that was corn fields on someone elses land. We decided to do a ghost box session which is a device that runs white noise between radio stations where voices come through to communicate with us. It didn't take long to pick up something up on the device that made my hair stand up. The voice that came through was a males voice and it said "Watchers." It was captured close to the barn and I recalled what the show Dead Files said. They had mentioned that there was something on the land that watches people that live there. So just hearing that voice gave me chill since it matched what was said on the show.

We gathered our things and went inside to talk with the owner before she left since she had no intentions of staying there anymore. The side door opened into a living room with hardwood floors and to the right was the kitchen. Just off the kitchen was a staircase that went up to the attic and behind that staircase was the entrance to the basement. The front of the house had three bedrooms and the attic area which was half finished had four bedrooms. The other part of the attic was storage and had blow insulation. It looked like it was blown into really big piles and it didn't make a whole lot of sense the way it was done and it was still freezing to the point where we could see our breath. We ventured for a peek into the basement which was very old with a chamber that was once used for coal and the bricks or fieldstone in some spots was all cemented together. There was one room that frightened me and gave me chills. The entrance was so low that you had to duck down to get inside and there were no windows, well there was a window or something and it was now cemented over and looked out of place. I felt trapped when I walked into that room something just didn't feel right. It got a little more intense when the owner said come upstairs I want to show you something. We headed back upstairs to one of the bedrooms in the front of the house to a section in the floor where one of the boards was loose and she picked up the one board and said peek inside and tell me what you see. I looked inside and there was a room under the floor that also had hardwood floors and of course was empty but none the less it was a room under the house that was not visible from the basement. I thought about it for a second and then it came to me that this room was on the other side of the room in the basement that had the window cemented over. Lily said they found it by accident while moving some furniture. Lily said before your team goes back downstairs to check it out more I will show you the shop and the things we found in the wall. I didn't realize that the red building next to the house was part of the dwelling too. She said it used to be a ice-cream shop a long time ago with old-fashioned ice cream. We entered through a door off the livingroom into the shop which had tons of tools and tractors still waiting to be moved to their new location. The books and the newspaper clippings were all sitting out on the table for us to look through along with the corset from what had to been a very tiny women since I couldn't even get it around my leg. The newspaper clippings were very old dating back to the 1800s. I noticed off to the right side of the shop a cement ramp going down to a sliding door. That door went down into the basement of the house to bring stuff down from the shop rather than going into the house first. Well now we all had a good layout of what we would be investigating and Lily said she was going to head out so we could find out what was still residing in the darkness.

We grabbed all our gear. John had a voice recorder and a thermal imager. Lloyd and I had voice recorders, ghost-box, and video cameras. Celena had a K2 meter and voice recorder. Our first stop was the attic so we headed upstairs. There was tons of left over stuff that the owner said they were just going to toss out. The beams of the attic were made from logs. There was haze that I didn't notice before up there which we noted was coming from the blown insulation and was floating in the air. I said my sinuses were bothering me as the air seemed thick. We asked some questions in the dark to try to find out if anything would respond to us. We heard a loud knock come from in front of us but we could see nothing. John said he had nothing visible on the thermal camera at all. I heard a loud knock to my left on what sounded like the wall but again nothing was seen. We stayed up there for about half hour and was about to head downstairs when we heard a loud crash come from the first floor followed by footsteps running down more stairs. We all looked at each other and headed down to the first floor to see what it was but of course nothing was there. I know what we had to do and we all seemed reluctant as the sound of the footsteps we heard running from us headed downstairs to the basement and that is where we needed to go. The thought of the hidden room came into my mind and how I felt in the room adjacent to it.

We made our way down to the basement, and Lloyd and I sat on some chairs just outside the room that was all cement with no windows. John and Celena stayed by the stairs that we had just come down to listen for footsteps or noises. I started asking questions to why they were there or why they insisted on tormenting the owners of the home. It didn't take long for something to happen. The room where Lloyd and I were sitting by jumped into play when we both got hit with this massive draft of air that came from within the room like something was leaving the area. It was a cold night but the air that came out of the room was like *ice ripping our veins open*. There were no windows and that room was solid cement so whatever was in there was now in the open basement. We kinda all looked at each other and wondered what would happen next. Celena thought she heard the steps creek in front of her and she must have been right because we were now hearing something upstairs. So whatever came out of that room was now on the first floor. We heard it moving around up there and things sliding across the floor and what we thought might have been a scream.

The room with no windows and sealed opening to hidden room The Attic

My next course of action was to yell up the stairs in the darkness to tell the ghost to come back down and talk to us. John was holding the thermal camera up toward the top of the stairs in hopes it would make an appearance. Our hopes were turned to terror when John and Celena jumped back away from the stairs and loud footsteps started coming down toward us. We all saw on the thermal this cold mass of a person coming down toward us but could only make out that it was a tall person. We all backed way off and let it wander into the basement. It made its way to a door of a room that was the old coal chamber and dissapeared into the darkness of that room and the thermal now showed nothing. We all went toward the darkness of the room where it went. I peeked into the darkeness when suddenly a loud growl pierced my ears and we all heard it. That was as close as I was getting to that room at the moment and shining our flashlights into the room showed nothing but a empty room. We were all a little on edge now so we stepped back away from the room into the middle of the basement. Celena noted that it was now much colder than it had been before. We stayed down there long enough to hear some bangs and scraping sounds coming from the coal room. To me it sounded like fingernails on cement. It stopped suddenly and nothing more was heard. We decided to head back upstairs to check out the shop.

We headed to the shop where all the stuff that the owners had found in the wall was laying out on the table. We wanted to see if anything was curious while we were going through the items and reading the clippings. All was quiet except for a few knocks and bangs near the wall. It was pretty quiet so our last stop of the night was going to be the attic. We ventured back up to the attic and the haze from the blown insulation seemed to be getting thicker. We only heard a few more faint noises and everything seemed to get quiet. We decided to call it a night and some of us had a headache from the haze and dust. We took some final pictures before heading out of the house. The pictures picked up lots of dust but nothing out of the ordinary.

I called the owners the next day to tell them of what had happened in the basement and they were not surprised as it's one of the areas that they least like to go. Whatever was down there was not too friendly and like to do quite a bit of stopping around. We would have loved to go back again but they have since moved out and not sure of the current owners or if it was rented out again.

CHAPTER 2

SALLIE HOUSE
ATCHISON, KANSAS

By Melissa Clevenger

The Sallie House

Part of my passion as a paranormal investigator is the history of the places, we get the opportunity to investigate. I began to build my own personal bucket list of haunted locations that I dreamed to go to. Toward the top of my bucket list was none other than the well-known Sallie House. When a tour became available for this location, I had no choice but to jump on the opportunity. The bonus of this investigation was that it was in Kansas which just happens to be my home state. We scheduled our trip for June which I knew would be very hot for Kansas. Investigators on this trip included Travis, and our two good friends from Minnesota Heather and Kristin. We began our nine-hour and thirty-six-minute drive to Kansas which really didn't seem to bad due to my excitement. Upon arrival we met up with Heather and Kristin at a restaurant for some dinner before our long night. Our investigation was to start at 7 p.m. and would go until 5 a.m. We were all beyond excited.

The Sallie House History

Atchison is known to be one of the most historical and scenic towns in Kansas. Through the years it has also became known as one of the most haunted towns, and the Sallie House has become known as one of the most haunted houses in America. The house was built somewhere around 1867 and belonged to the Finney family for over a century. Mr. Finney was a doctor who used the front of the house as his office space and examination room for his patients. The family used the remainder of the house as their living quarters which was quite common in those days. The story that has been passed down through the years is that one day a mother came rushing in through the front door of the house with her young daughter draped over her arms. The young girl named Sallie had been suffering from severe abdominal pains. Dr. Finney quickly diagnosed the little girl with appendicitis, and he feared that her appendix would soon burst. Immediate surgery was the only answer. In fact, Dr. Finney made the surgery so immediate that he began cutting on the poor little girl before she was even sedated. Agonizing screams could be heard as he proceeded with the surgery. Soon the screams suddenly stopped as she died right there on the operating table. After the Finney family moved out a single woman moved in and lived in the house for the next forty years with no problems to report.

In 1993 Tony and Debra Pickman rented out the house to begin their family. They welcomed a son who they named Taylor. Soon after moving in paranormal activity began. Tony's first encounter was in the kitchen one night when he went to get a drink and he saw a little girl just standing there staring at him. After this the haunting became more intense. The family dog would growl at thin air. Debra and Tony would here noises coming from the nursery, toys would rearrange themselves, fires broke out in the house, pictures were known to turn upside down, lights would turn off and on just to name some of the activity. Tony Pickman began to be physically attacked and was receiving burns and scratches on his body. After two years in the house the Pickman family could not take any more of the hauntings and they moved out. It has been said that Sallie attacks men in the house to get revenge on the doctor who botched her surgery. Through the years the Sallie House has received national attention from television shows and paranormal investigators.

The Investigation of the Sallie House

As we pull up to the notorious Sallie House, we can't help but think of all the stories we have heard from this place. Is this house going to live up to our expectations? The first thing I notice is the great big two-story house across the street with big bright porch lights on. It seemed so welcoming and I couldn't help but think of the family inside enjoying their quiet evening not even knowing what we would be doing across the street. Stepping out of the car my breath is taken away by the deadness in the air. The humidity is so high for a summer day in Kansas that at first it stops me in my tracks. We had to watch every step we took on the sidewalk due to the unevenness of each slab. Before I realized it, we were there. The Sallie House sat there right in front of me. At first glance the house appeared rather small. Paint was peeling from the siding. We walked up onto the front porch and into the living room. The energy in the house feels very compact. It is hard to determine if the energy is either good or bad. We begin our night with a brief tour of the house to get accustomed before the lights go out. The dining room would become our base area where we would keep all our equipment. It is now time for lights out. In pure darkness the house begins to feel even smaller. Due to my research of the house I already knew the key areas that I wanted to investigate. To begin our investigation, we set up in the main bedroom. This bedroom was made up as if occupants still lived in the house. The small dark closet seemed like an inviting place for Travis to set up with a voice recorder.

I decided to set up camp on the bed across the room. We had been sitting in our positions in the bedroom for a good forty-five minutes with absolutely nothing happening. I began to worry that our night would be a bust. Even the ghost box that we were using was silent with the occasional radio station coming through. Suddenly I felt a burning sensation below my neck. Right away I said that I thought I had been scratched. I burnt bad and what I found odd was that the burning feeling was coming from under my skin. Kristin grabbed her flashlight and pointed the light at me and sure enough there was a large scratch. As she was looking at the scratch the ghost box said, "Scratched her!" Then it said scratch again and right at that time Travis blurted out that he had been scratched. Travis explained it the same way as if he was burning from underneath his skin. Shortly after the ghost box said, "Scratch Heather." We patiently waited to see if Heather would be scratched as well, but luckily, she was not. With enough of getting scratched we decided to pack up our gear and head to the basement. Before we could make it out of the bedroom the wind outside fiercely picked up. Lightning was almost nonstop, and the thunder crashed through the sky. As we looked at our phones for the weather, we realized we were in store for a huge storm with the possibility for tornados. What a way to investigate and add to the eerie feeling of the house. After waiting out the storm for a little while we decided to continue our journey to the basement. We headed down the stairs, through the living room, and into the kitchen with the red cabinets where the basement door was. The basement was very much like the old scary basements that I was used to seeing in Kansas. The four of us sat on chairs, turned on our laser grid, and our voice recorders. We decided to begin our time in the basement with a ghost box session. The nice thing in the basement was that no radio stations were coming through at all. The first thing we asked was what is your name? The response we received was a rather scary males voice that said "Jesus." Shortly after a female voice said, "I love you," which was followed by a male voice saying "I love you" back to her. I honestly will never forget the female and male saying I love you to each other. Just thinking about it is amazing, even in death the couple proclaimed their love for each other. Well enough about love, the rest of our ghost box session involved what could have been a little girl whispering all her answers. We asked what her name was and the response we received was a little girl whispering "Sallie." Were we communicating with Sallie, the little girl who tragically died in the house so many years ago? It got to be almost everything we asked the little girl would whisper just loud enough where we could all hear her "Sallie." I then asked Sallie why was she whispering, was she scared of something? The response was once again a whisper, but she said "yes!" What was Sallie so afraid of? We began to feel that we had a mystery on our hands that we needed to solve. Did Sallie need our help? There was an area in the basement that we were a little leery of so I said should I go over there. The ghost box replied with "walk over." Heather asked Sallie how old she was and right on cue the laser grid turned off and on seven times. I am not positive on how old Sallie was when she passed away. We then asked is they knew what year it was, and the ghost box said, "I forgot." We tried several area's in the house with not much happening. Most of our night was spent in the basement where we had amazing ghost box sessions.

The stairs to second floor

The weathered look of the Sallie House

I have heard from several people that the house had been cleansed and was no longer haunted. I would have to disagree with them. Sallie obviously wanted us to hear her name. The night that we spent at the Sallie House there were too many people in the house investigating. I plan on going back to the Sallie House someday to investigate again with no more than five people. We ended our night just shy of 5 a.m. unable to stay awake any longer to investigate. Leaving the house, I still could not tell if the energy in the house was either good or bad, that part will remain a mystery to me.

CHAPTER 3

GROPPI'S
BAY VIEW, WISCONSIN

By Craig Nehring

Groppi's in Bay View

Groppi's grocery store has so much history that one knows not where to even start. We will start first with the reason I wanted to investigate this unique location. I was born in Milwaukee and when I was young my Father would take me down to Jones Island by the railroad tracks to watch trains just a few blocks down from the store. My love for trains became a daily routine after school but not before stopping at Al's Custard Stand for a chocolate malt a place that is gone now swallowed up by the many car lots around town.

In 2003 my brother John Nehring along with his Wife Anne Finch Nehring bought the store from the Groppi family which operated the store in 1923. John would tell me that stuff would happen in the store like groceries were moved from the shelf and would appear on the floor in different isles. He said some of the employees would see shadows in the basement and hear noises. John and Anne believe the ghosts that reside in the store are the former owners John, Louie, Mario, and possibly James Groppi who was a civil rights activist. It could be possible that they had the store set up a certain way and maybe they think the items are in the wrong spots and they move them. Employees have reported radios and lights turning on and off by themselves. One worker even saw a man standing in the store after closing time. She later identified the man as Louie Groppi from a 1965 photo. John would tell me of the trap door in the floor which is no longer in use but still visible to see. The trap door was used back in the day for when they made vinegar in the basement but that was just what they said. The reality was it was used for bootlegging and easy way to get it to the basement quickly. So, I really wanted to investigate here and my brother John owning it was a bonus.

The History of Groppi's

Groppi's was founded in 1913 by Italian immigrants Giocondo and Giorgina Groppi. The store is known as one of the oldest Italian food stores in the Milwaukee area. It was known for some of the best Italian food and homemade salami. The store had hardwood floors and not like today's linoleum floors. One of the coolers inside was made of wood and is still there today in use. James Groppi was born in 1930 and his parents immigrated from Italy. James grew up in the

Milwaukee area in the Bay View area and eleven brothers and sisters worked at his parent's grocery store. Mario Groppi passed away in 2002.

John and Anne purchased the store in 2003 and it opened on Thanksgiving. They added lots of new things like heating and plumbing but kept much of the store original like the hardwood floors. He kept the meat case and the old-fashioned cooler. He also kept the original counters up front dating back to 1913. The old photographs of the Groppi's still hang in the store.

The old-fashioned cooler with inside made of wood

The Tour of the Store Prior to Investigation

I have been to my brother's store many times but was never really given a tour and knew much about the history prior to this investigation. On this investigation was Kara, Melissa, and Celena and we were ready for the tour and the food that was going to follow because the food is so amazing there that it is almost better than a ghost hunt. We started by getting a tour of the front of the store where the old-fashioned counters and all the items that were sale behind it. The setup reminded me of watching the show Little

House on the Prairie where the customer would ask for something and they would pull it off the shelf and hand it to them just like this store here. We ventured down the isles to get a feel for where all the items were and then headed to the back of the store where the wine and bar was at. John showed us an old wooden door that hung on the ceiling which was the original door that came out of the Groppi's residence for every time they came out to the store to greet the customers. Below that door underneath the stacks of wine was a trap door, the door that originally led to the basement to where they would make vinegar or bootlegging in other words. It was sealed up from the basement covered over but you still can see where it is at by a black x that marks the spot on the ceiling in the basement. To the right of the wine is a bar where patrons can come and have some wine or other refreshments and further to the right was the meat and deli sections. We headed to the basement from there where even though the floorplan was small there were lots of little nooks and crannies. Now it was time to eat before the investigation.

The front end of the store

The Investigation of Groppi's

We got our equipment ready and decided we would start on the first floor back by the bar area. I was doing some video so Melissa and Celena were standing behind the bar to see if anything would talk to them. We started by asking questions, but it was quiet other than a few noises from further up in the store. It's an old store so since we were never there before it easily could have been normal everyday noises. I than had Melissa ask questions behind the bar to see if someone wanted to respond to a female instead of the male voice. It didn't take long when she had asked "Who is here with us." Melissa thought she heard a loud voice next to her, so I played back the audio and sure enough there was a voice there that was hard to make out, so I decided to enhance it a little bit. What we found was quite amazing a voice that said, "I am Groppi." This was the voice that Melissa heard to right of her like he whispered in her ear. So, was this one of the original owners of the store?

We decided to move up to the front of the store and sit behind the counters to see if we could hear footsteps or other noises. Our equipment we had wasn't doing to much or showing us that anything paranormal was around. I pulled out the ghost box to see if anyone wanted to communicate with us. We heard some voices, but they were hard to make out and would have to go over it when we got home. While I had the box going, we thought we heard something in one of the isles and walked over to that isle that we thought we heard it come from. Suddenly there was a loud sliding noise that came from above us and we all looked up. I caught a glimpse of the attic door moving with my flashlight and it stopped when I shined the light on it. Well that just gave me goosebumps and we clearly noticed the attic door on the tour earlier as I was going to ask what was up there but never did. I know at the time it was closed and now it sits slightly ajar. Wow! This just happened and we saw it, but the question was what was it? What moved the attic door aside and what came out or what went in was the question on our minds. So now I am thinking where it is and is it standing by us. We spent quite a bit of time in this area but nothing else was heard. It was getting late and we still needed to check out the basement, so we headed down there.

We started in the section right below the trap door. I was asking questions when Kara said she felt something pull her hair which was funny cause I thought something grabbed my pants leg but didn't say anything since I thought I had imagined it but now I was thinking maybe I didn't. Celena said that she thought she heard something up stairs move, and I thought maybe it was the attic door again. I said I was going to walk over one room, so we are not all standing together in one spot. While I waited in the room over on the other side of the wall, I told Melissa to ask some questions. As she was asking questions, I heard another loud noise upstairs but couldn't make out what part of the store it had come from.

We decided one more time upstairs to see if the attic had moved more but once we got up there it was still in its same location. All seemed to die down and no more noises was heard so we decided to call it a night. While going over evidence from the ghost box I discovered a voice while sitting by the counter and it said, "Go get Anne." Now was this a ghost talking about my brother's wife Anne. I captured a couple other faint voices but way too hard to hear so I didn't keep them. It was a very neat place to investigate and the attic door moving along with Kara and Celena getting touched was very interesting but still the voice that whispered in Melissa's ear that said I am Groppi tells me that he is still there watching over the place but whoever is there is friendly.

The bar where Melissa heard a voice whisper in her ear

CHAPTER 4

PRESTON RESIDENCE MARQUETTE, KANSAS

By Melissa Clevenger

The Preston House

After scheduling an investigation at the Sallie House I was excited to be able to finally go back to Marquette to visit my friends and family that I hadn't seen in years. From Atchison, Marquette was only a three-hour drive. Travis and I woke up early from our hotel to begin our trip to Marquette.

My brother Eric had been gone for twenty-two years and in all those years I had not been able to communicate with him. Travis and I decided that we would do a full investigation of my dad's house. The funny thing was that my dad was in Wisconsin watching our house for us so that we could go to Kansas. This was the perfect opportunity for us to have the house to ourselves.

Finally, making it to Main Street in Marquette I could feel my excitement to see my childhood home. We made it to the stop sign and only had a right turn to make before we were there. My emotions were mixed on what to expect investigating my dad's house. To contact my brother and maybe get some answers would be amazing. Only the night could tell what was in store for us.

The History of the Preston Residence

Marquette, Kansas is a small farming town that was named after Marquette, Michigan. In 1873, Marquette began with a flourmill that was located on the banks of the Smoky Hill River. The downtown area of Marquette has a historical feel to it with Victorian style buildings that are listed on the Kansas State Register of Historic Places.

The parents of Howard and Kermit Peterson built what would later become the Preston residents in the early months of 1905. Howard and *Cecil* Peterson lived in the house and were the owners of the grocery store across the alley. In the backyard there was an underground freezer for storing food. *Cecil* was a dentist but he never pursued his career. Then in May of 1905 a devastating tornado ripped through the town leveling almost the entire community. Very few houses survived the tornado however the Peterson's house still stood.

In 1977, Larry and Brenda Preston purchased the house along with their new son Eric. The house was perfect for the new family with nine rooms and five bedrooms, and Marquette was the perfect little town to raise kids in. The family was complete in June of 1979 with the birth of their daughter Melissa. The room that would become my room was completely full of dental equipment from the previous owners.

The haunted history of the Preston residents began with me when I was very young. The first memory that I have was when I was about five years old. We kept all our shoes at the end of the hallway right before the upstairs. My mom sent me to go get my shoes from the hallway, which was always scary for me as a child. As I approached the banister I peered up to the top of the stairs and sitting on the railing at the very top was Jesus' mom Mary. I don't know how I knew it was Mary sitting there but trust me I knew. She was beautiful and she just sat there silently, and then she gave me the sweetest purest smile you could ever imagine. I froze for a couple of minutes and could only stare back at her. Then the terror took over my body and I bolted down the hallway back to where my mom stood. I never told my parents about this experience, but I do believe that Mary gave me my gift of being able to see and hear spirits. This would be one of my first of many experiences in this house.

I could write an entire book on my experiences in my house growing up, but with only having a chapter I will let you hear my most memorable stories. It was very common for me to see ghost in my house, in fact, it was daily. The ghost did not always interact with me for the most part it was like they didn't even see me. On several occasions I saw two ghosts walk past my bedroom door and they looked like they were just walking and talking to each other. They never even bothered to look at me. That's the thing with this house, there was no shortage of spirits and they carried on as if they were just passing through.

One night when I was about nine years old a young boy prob-ably around ten years old rose from the side of my bed. He had an antique look to him. The boy was lying flat with his arms to his side and he was looking straight up. His body rose from the side of my bed closest to the closet and he rose all the way up and through the ceiling. Another night I was facing my closet and there was an old scary man lying in the bed next to me. The man was at least eighty years old and I could tell he was a ghost although he looked human. I hid under my covers and was terrified. Several scarier things would happen in the years to come from between my bed and the closet. From that point forward I never faced the closet when I went to bed or when I slept.

Anytime I would have sleepovers at my house with friends something would usually happen to scare us. We often would sneak out late in the night to go play in the local park. On one night my brother and I and two other friends were creeping across the living room to sneak out when we heard my mom Brenda yell at us to get back to bed. All four of us turned to face my mom and saw her standing right behind us. Before we could answer her, she faded away. This was not the first time that my mom appeared to us or yelled at us only to disappear. One morning I heard my mom yell from her bedroom at me to get the cat out of the laundry basket. There was a laundry basket full of clothes in the hallway, but no cat in it. I walked into my mother's bedroom to tell her and she was not there. I then went into the bathroom to take a shower and after a few minutes in there the shower door flew open and slammed back shut. This was when I realized that I was all alone in the house. Activity typically would be very severe when I was home alone. When others where in the house with me the ghost were all around but would pretty much keep to themselves. When they knew that I was alone however doors would slam and voices were loud.

Fast forward to April 30, 1997. I remember every detail of that day as if it were yesterday. My parents had gotten a divorce, so my mom lived in Wisconsin at this time. My brother and I had scheduled nights to talk to my mom on the phone. This night was not one of the scheduled nights, but for some reason my brother and I had to call my mom so we could each talk to her. After hanging up my brother went to his girlfriend's house for about an hour. That night I was excited to watch The Ellen Degeneres show, it was her coming out episode which was unheard of in those days. Right before the show was to begin, I went to walk into the kitchen. When I got to the doorway my brother Eric was just standing there. He looked like a ghost, and I never heard him come in the door. I told him he scared me, but I will never forget how he looked like a ghost. My brother then watched the entire show with me which was a rare occasion.

May 1, 1997. Yet another day I will never forget. I remember getting ready for school and walking in the kitchen to see a note on the table. My brother needed my dad to go to the bank and make his truck payment for him. My school day was typical until I got to government class. I sat at my desk and I just knew that something was wrong. I stood up and sat down probably twenty times. I didn't know what to do, I knew something was wrong and I needed to call home, but I didn't know what to tell my teacher.

Finally, the end of the school day, as I got onto the school bus my horrible feeling continued to get even worse. By this time, I felt that I was probably going to die on my way home. I truly thought that somehow, I was going to die. As I walked up to my house, I saw people there and I just knew something was terribly wrong. I walked in the house and my dad took me into the dining room and told me to sit in the wooden rocking chair because he had something that he needed to tell me. This was the moment my life would change and would never be the same. My brother Eric worked for a construction company. He was placing flags along the road to create the path for the new road. As he was placing the flags a guy in an earth mover was coming from behind. For some reason, that we may never know, the guy decided to turn the machine and drive away. Nobody even realized what happened they kept working. Somebody then realized my brother was laying in the mud face down. I lost my only brother Eric on May 1, 1997.

The headstone of Melissa's brother

After my brother died and before the funeral, several family members where coming from out of state. I was upset because I needed to get clean sheets for everyone, and I could not find any. My brother's door had a latch lock at the very top of the door. As I was standing in front of his door upset about the sheets the lock lifted and unlocked. I decided to look in my brothers' room because there had to be some reason for the door to unlock. Sitting right there clean and folded at the end of his bed sat a stack of clean sheets. I never doubted that he wasn't there.

Shortly after Eric's death, I had a dream about him. In my dream I walked out of my house and walked to the end of the sidewalk. When I looked across the street, I saw my brother walking toward me from the grocery store. He walked up to me as if nothing was wrong. At first, I was so happy to see him and all I could do was hug him. Then I realized that he was not supposed to be alive, so I pushed him away. I asked my brother why he was there because he was not supposed to be alive.

A few weeks later I had another dream about my brother Eric. In this dream I was at the elementary school that we went to as kids. I walked by the library and sitting there was my brother. He looked at me and smiled and waved. He was probably about ten years old in this dream and he was wearing a baby blue t-shirt that I remember him wearing when he was younger. I have thought about those dreams many times through the years. I truly believe that my brother came back to me in a dream as a child because of how I reacted to him when he came to me at the age of his death.

Not long after my brother Eric's death I went away to college and then a few years later moved to Wisconsin. My dad continues to live in the house, to this day, all alone. I try to go back to Kansas to visit when I can. As far as a haunted house, I can say that this house is truly haunted.

The Investigation of the Preston Residence

This investigation was like no other for me. I have been on numerous investigations in many states, this investigation however was very personal. I prayed that my brother would come through to us. Slowly I stepped out of our vehicle and onto the grass examining every detail of the house I grew up in. A house full of so many memories, and now that was all they were, memories.

In the yard sat my brother's red Chevy Silverado truck. All these years have passed and still it sat for its owner to never return to it. The house that was glorious many years ago, now desperately needed a paint job. As I looked up, I can't help but notice my brother's bedroom window. "Please let us know you are here tonight Eric, please."

Travis and I finally reach the front door and unlock it to take our first step in years into the old house. In the living room the first thing I walk up to is the wall by the couch. I run my hand across all the gashes in the wall through the wallpaper. When I was younger my brother was into karate. When our parents were working, he would throw flying stars at me and they would stick in the wall. Thankfully he had very good aim since his goal was to scare me, not actually hit me. All these years and so much has remained the same, I am finally home.

I decided it was time to begin our investigation, night was falling upon us. Travis opened the hallway door to head upstairs as I briefly paused reminiscing on one of my first experiences as a child. Up the stairs we went and began to get out the gear that we planned on using that night. I wanted to set a recorder somewhere upstairs, so I walked over to my old bedroom door and opened the door. I asked Travis where I should go, and we wouldn't know it until later, but we had a perfect EVP that said, "In here."

We then unlocked and opened my brother's door to his bedroom. Twenty-two years without him here yet his room has not changed at all. The bed is still made the way he had it with the same sheets. The calendar on the wall is still set at April 1997. He died on May 1st, so the calendar was never changed to May. His shelves identical to how he left them. Swords crossed on the wall, a pyramid of Skoal chew cans taking up an entire shelf. His drawers still contain all his clothes folded and put away neatly. Every detail of Eric's room is the way he left it. Surprisingly after all these years his room only needed a good dusting.

The Skoal Chew cans still in their same spot

I decided it would be best to conduct our investigation in the upstairs hallway right in front of my brother's door. In this loca-tion we would be able to see anything that went on in all directions. The upstairs hallway was also where I saw most of the ghost when I was growing up. I sat my voice recorder right in front of me on the floor. We began by asking basic questions such as "who is here with us tonight." Travis continued with this type of questions for a few minutes. Nothing, the house for the first time ever was completely silent. No creeks, no shadows, no voices, just silence.

Travis then decided we should give the ghost box a shot. It felt like this was the time we should try to communicate with my brother Eric. We began by asking Eric if he was here. The ghost box was quiet, not a single radio station was coming through, the box was almost as quiet as the house. Travis then asked, "Who lived in this house?" I heard the ghost box say "dad," but that was all that I heard. So, I said "yes, your dad does live here." Several more questions, and still no responses at all.

This house has never been this quiet, I could not understand. A bit frustrated because my hopes were so high, we decided to call it a night rather early. We were staying with Travis' sister Andrea in McPherson so this was the end of our physical investigation. I brought Boo Bear along, so I decided we would leave the bear in the hallway overnight along with a voice recorder. Boo Bear is an actual bear that asks EVP questions, monitors temperature, sound, and movement. I would not know my results from my recordings of Boo Bear until the ride home to Kansas when I would listen to my audio.

Boo Bear device for ghost hunting

Walking out of my childhood house was very emotional for me. This was the house that ultimately made me who I am. The memories made in this house shaped the person I am today. Although many of my memories in this house were rather scary, they gave me purpose. The ghosts of the past were always with me and continue to follow me to this day. As I turned to close the front door, I momentarily peeked my head in the house to say goodbye to my brother. Even though we didn't hear him, I just knew he was there with us.

The rest of our trip in Marquette was nice. Travis and I had a chance to meet up with a very dear friend of mine and I cherish the time we had. It was rather sad leaving Marquette since I didn't know when I would be able to come back to visit. Heading home back to Wisconsin we decided we would drive the twelve-hour drive straight through since we both would have to work the next day.

Once I was comfortable in the passenger seat, I pulled out my laptop, recorder, and headphones to begin listening to my audio from the prior night's investigation at my dad's house. Luckily, I had a full charge on my laptop because this was going to be a very long drive home.

I decided to work backward on my audio. I started listening first to my overnight recording at my dads of Boo Bear. Boo Bear would ask a question, pause briefly to wait for a response, and then would ask a different question. Boo Bear must have had a full charge on her batteries because she lasted all night long asking questions. This part of the audio was very boring because with every question asked there was nothing but silence to follow it. In fact, I listened to over fourteen hours of questions followed by silence. I was very disappointed in this. I thought for sure that the house would come alive once we left it alone, and boy was I wrong.

Once I managed to get through the audio of Boo Bear, I was ready to listen to the investigation that Travis and I had conducted earlier that night. The beginning, where we were asking questions was completely silent. I then got to the part where we did the ghost box session. I knew when we were investigating that the ghost box was quiet with no radio stations so I really thought I would be wasting my time listening to the audio, but I decided since we still had such a long drive, I would listen to it anyway.

The first question Travis asked was "who lived in this house." I heard my brother respond, "Me, you, dad, Preston." This was true, before my brother died, I lived in the house with my brother and my dad and our last name was Preston. I then said, "That is right dad does live here." I gave that response because with my ears at the time I only heard "Dad." I couldn't believe it, after twenty-two years I had finally connected with my brother and I didn't even know it when we were investigating.

After the first response on the ghost box there was an even greater message. My brother said, "Sorry was killed, Eric messed up." I listened to my brother repeatedly in amazement. We did not hear anything when we were in the house investigating and the ghost box was silent, yet on my recording I had a message from my brother Eric that meant so much to me.

My brother Eric was killed on May 1, 1997, while working his construction job. One of the workers had turned the Earth Mover and ran him over and left him there not even knowing what he had done. For twenty-two years I blamed this man for my brother's death. Twenty-two years is such a long time to not let something go. My brother's message saying, "Sorry was killed, Eric messed up," was what I needed to hear. Eric was telling me to not blame that guy for his death anymore. This was the first time that I truly forgave the guy who I thought caused us so much sorrow.

My trip was complete, I finally communicated with my brother Eric. I miss him with all my heart, and I will forever miss him. I now know that I can communicate with my brother everywhere, he is always with us. Our loved ones who we have lost can be anywhere at any time. It brings peace to me just knowing that even after all these years my brother is still with us. This investigation was the most personal one I have ever done, and I am glad I finally had the opportunity to do it.

To my brother Eric, you always meant the world to me. As children we would go on magical adventures, you had a way of making the story books come alive. Thank you for being not only my brother but also my friend. Now that you are gone, I have learned to create adventures of my own, but I know that you are always with me. I will love you forever and always Eric until we meet again someday.

Eric Preston November 23, 1976 to May 1, 1997

CHAPTER 5

POASTTOWN ELEMENTARY SCHOOL
POASTTOWN, OHIO

By Craig Nehring

Poasttown School

I wanted to choose from two haunted locations for one trip out of state so the first one that I picked was Poasttown School in Ohio as I heard from others it was extremely haunted. We had Travis, Kara, and Korin on this investigation. It seems like the trip to these places is half the fun; however, this time not so much. We got down there a day early so we stayed in a hotel in Indiana and I was about to dose off when I thought something bit me on the leg. I brushed it off as my imagination and tried to go back to bed. A moment later I felt something bite my elbow and I woke up and yelled to Kara in the other bed that something was biting me, and we should check the covers to make sure there is nothing there. We turned on the lights and pulled the covers back to find adult bedbugs in the sheets among other bugs I couldn't identify. I messaged Travis who was in the other room and his room had the same bugs. Well by this time I had welts on my skin and choose to sleep in Kara's car the rest of the night while the others choose the top of the blankets. I reported the bugs to the front desk the next morning and was able to get my room for free, but the damage was already done with itching and red welts that would last three weeks on my skin.

Onward down the road we went to our first destination. We arrived early on while it was still light to get some pictures before dark. Korin was not with us and would be arriving later in the night because I think she drove to the wrong state by mistake. Prior to our investigation I did some reading online to try to find the hot spots in the school so we could locate where to investigate. The gym was said to be very active and a stairwell where a little girl had fallen to her death. There was also activity in the hallways and a room where lots of dolls were collected.

The History of Poasttown School

The School opened in 1937 and closed in 2000 and some of the beliefs behind the hauntings are said to possibly caused by a railway accident. The Middletown rails were pretty treacherous in the late 1800s into the 1900s. On July 25, 1891, employees of National Cash Register were on their way back up to Dayton from their company picnic. Their passenger train collided with a freight train causing four deaths and fifty injuries.

On July 4, 1910, there was a horrific train accident that occurred when an engineer of the Big Four passenger train ran off schedule after a detour. This caused mass chaos and when the second train, full of freight, saw the original train it was too late. All passengers in the two cars closest to the engine either died or were seriously injured. There were nineteen deaths at the scene of the accident, and countless others who were hurt. There were no hospitals at the time, so the land where the school currently sits, was used as a makeshift triage. Relief trains were sent out, and the passengers who survived were taken to hospitals in other nearby cities. In the end, there were a total of thirty-six deaths.

The other possible cause for the hauntings may have been because of a flood. Most of Butler County was a scene of mass destruction due to the great flood of 1913. It swept through cities with a vengeance, and six people were killed just outside of the city of Middletown. However, the flood destroyed so many homes and businesses in the area that it may have left some residual energy behind as well.

There is one other theory our team always stands by is the fact the ghosts tend to like to hang where they loved to be like as in school. The kids may have loved this school and their friends they would hang out with, so if you're a ghost wouldn't you like to be where your favorite memories were at. We always encounter ghosts of children in most of the schools that we have investigated so why would this one be any different.

The Investigation

We started the investigation without Korin as she was not even in Ohio yet. Our first spot was the doll room and there were tons of dolls from the bottom of the wall and on shelves for the length of the entire room and then when we walked into the next room there were even more dolls. I was doing some video recording and as I walked by one of dolls I noticed that it's eyes were following me and I did a step back to check the doll out only to find out the dolls eyes were stationary, so how did they follow me or was it just my imagination. We continued into the next room where I stood on one end to video tape and Travis and Kara sat in some chairs apart from one another. We asked some questions in the dark and heard some small knocks. I was standing up still using the video camera and I thought something had grabbed my leg. Kara also has said that she thought she felt something touch her hair but after that all was quiet. We decided to head down the hallway a little bit to a staircase that a little girl was rumored to have fallen to her death. When we got there, we could hear some dogs barking at the neighbor's house and they were loud, and we had to wait to ask questions in-between the barks. At one point when I asked a question if the little girl was there, we heard what sounded like shuffling at the bottom of the staircase. Is it possible this was the little girl moving around at the bottom of the staircase? The noise ended with what we thought was a loud scream maybe even a girl screaming. All was quiet then other than the dogs that continued and certainly wasn't going to stop. Travis said there was no way we were going to hear anything more, so we decided to take a break and head back to basecamp.

The top of staircase looking down where the girl was to have fallen

We were back at basecamp which consisted of a huge classroom with lots of beds that we would stay the night in. Korin had finally arrived and it was midnight now which left us still some decent time to investigate yet. We headed up to a classroom where one of the teachers was not the nicest to the kids to see if we could capture something up there. I was again using the video camera, so I hung outside the classroom while Travis and Kara and Korin sat inside the room by the desks. It was pitch black and I decided to try something I usually try at haunted locations and that is to yell out Marco in hopes something would yell back. I yelled it out and thought I heard something say Polo back close to me in the hallway. I then tried shave and a haircut which is a series of knocks that would be followed by two knocks back. Just as I finished the knocks came two knocks back, but they came from inside the room on the chalkboard next to Travis, but they were loud enough for all of us to hear. Travis and I at the exact same time said WTF was that and all of us were like wow the knocks were on cue. I tried it one more time, but nothing happened this time. I decided to wander off down to another level and left them three in the room. I went a few floors below down to the gym area to see if I could hear anything and get far enough away from them so they couldn't hear me. It was quiet in the gym and you could hear the traffic from outside on the main road. I was maybe down there for about an hour when I heard the rest of the team headed back to the basecamp area. I met back up with them and Kara said they were hearing footsteps out in the hallway by the classroom they were sitting in, but they were unable to see anything.

Our last stop of the night would be the gym since that is supposed to be one of the more haunted locations in the school. However, it became clear the ghosts did not want to join in the activity so we just made the best of it and played some basketball in hopes we could pick up some voices later. We also had a few hours journey to head to our second destination on the trip in the morning.

The gym at Poasttown School

CHAPTER 6

RANDOLPH COUNTY ASYLUM
WINCHESTER, INDIANA

By Craig Nehring

Randolph Asylum

The second stop on our two-night investigation is the Randolph County Asylum in Winchester Indiana and I heard many awesome reports to haunted activity here. Since we were at the school the night before, our drive over here was not so bad, and no bedbug infested hotels would be needed. We had the same crew other than Kevin and his wife was joining us for this investigation for the night.

The History of Randolph County Asylum

The county home, originally the Randolph County Poorhouse, was built in 1899. The property at one time included a pump house, two different barns, a machine shed, two garages as well as a chicken house. The property also has an unmarked cemetery somewhere on the grounds where some former residents of the poorhouse were buried.

Some of land purchased by county in 1851 was to house a poor farm to care for those unable to work, including the mentally and physically disabled, single mothers, elderly, and orphans. Dwelling existed on premises that served as facility for a time, then serving thirteen inmates. Residents were to maintain the farm, though many unable to perform labor due to age or infirmity.

In January of 1851 a fire destroyed the property and a new building was built in 1856 only to be demolished due to poor conditions and a newer construction process was used to build it to accommodate the growing population.

New nearly 50,000-square-foot building (current structure) constructed in 1898–1899. Housed six large wards, several private rooms, laundry, kitchen, separate dining rooms for women and men. Property included pump house, barn, hay barn, machine shed, garage or cell house, two garages, and chicken house on 350 acres. Cemetery also located on property, 230 yards northwest of the home.

In 1994, there was new ownership and it was called Countryside Care Center and it housed twelve residents.

It closed in 2008–2009 and became a storage facility for the county.

Current owners purchased from county in 2016 for reuse as paranormal attraction. Cemetery Neff Cemetery (also called White-Kelley or Randolph County Infirmary Cemetery) located north of infirmary on hill in middle of pasture field. Cemetery for White and Kelley families.

At least fifty unmarked graves reported located on property. Proposal in 1938 by descendant of John Neff sought to erect a fence around several of the oldest Neff family gravesites. Historical Society reset as many headstones as could be found in 1985.

Tragedies on the property consist of unknown number of deaths during infirmary's history; one estimate of 200. Number of tuberculosis deaths; a resident pushed out of a second-floor window; and hangings also believed reported.

A Miss Mary J. Blair lately died in the poor asylum, shortly after giving birth to a child. Before her death she wrote a note and addressed it to a man named A.H. Green, of West Liberty, Ohio, who afterwards confessed to be the father of the child. He professed to having been ignorant of the whereabouts of the woman during her stay in the asylum.

Sam Preston, inmate, lately tried to commit suicide by driving a penknife blade into his head with a flat iron. The doctor pulled out the blade and Sam failed.

The list and stories go on and on but now getting down to business we were about to take a tour and then on to the investigation.

The Tour of Randolph County Asylum

When you walk through the front doors there are two large rooms carpeted where we made one of them our basecamp. There is a kitchen just off the one room and then a long hallway that goes to other rooms. There is staircase just after the kitchen that leads upstairs to some more carpeted rooms with beds where we would be crashing after the investigation. There is also a stairway in the kitchen that leads to the basement that I didn't know was there till I came up from the basement during the investigation. Once at the top floor you walk out into the main wings that once housed the patients and there is a long hallway with rooms but if you were to take a step to the right just past the wall there is another long hallway that mirrors the first hallway with rooms on the right and it looks rather confusing at times almost like a funhouse. At then end of each wing there is a day room or sunroom for the patients. Each room has a little cutout hole at the top of the wall that was so back in the day when they had gas lamps the smoke would go up and out into the hallways instead of stay confined to the room. We noticed at the end of the hall in one of the sunrooms an old-fashioned light hung from the ceiling called a gas light. The second floor pretty much mimics the first floor and the massive attic took over the rest of the asylum. The basement also had long corridors that went on what seemed like forever and rooms that were just off in different directions. There was a room down there where a patient liked to hammer nails into the desk and screws and all types of things. If he could get it pounded into wood, he would do it. It is said now his ghost stands in that same room still trying to pound nails and stuff into the wood long after he has been gone.

One of the long hallways with the rooms on the side

The Investigation of the Asylum

I wanted to start in the basement for the investigation but Kevin and his wife had just gotten there and everyone wanted to order pizza before we started so while someone left to go pick it up I ventured down into the basement alone which at the time seemed like a great idea. The asylum lives up to its name for being haunted as I only made it down the stairs to one side of the hall when I heard footsteps coming toward me in the dark. I flipped on the flashlight and they stopped right in front of me. It was quiet but really wanted to turn off the light and see what happened. I instead turned around walked a few steps back toward the staircase and turned off the light. I stood close to my comfort zone knowing I could just go up the stairs to where everyone was at. I didn't hear anything else and had no clue where the ghost or whatever it was is at now. I decided to head back up to wait for pizza but as I got halfway up the stairs figured out where the ghost was. He was right behind me as I could hear the stairs creak one by one behind me and a thought popped into my head what if the door at the top of the stairs was locked and its right behind me what do I do then? I went up the stairs quick without turning around and bolted through the door to see Korin and Kara standing there. I told them what had happened and said I will wait till there is more than just me in the basement to investigate.

Now the pizza had arrived, and I hadn't noticed Korin had wandered off but saw her come out of the kitchen white as a ghost. She said she ventured down the stairs to see if she could hear what I heard and that something had followed her as well and up the same staircase as well. I told everyone I know where we are going and that is to the basement first stop. We all headed down there and stood in the long corridor of the basement. I set a REM Pod at one end down away from us close to the staircase that had the activity. The REM Pod is a device that creates its own magnetic field and if anything gets close to the device it would light up in different colors depending on the intensity. We all stood in the dark just waiting for the footsteps I heard earlier. It was pitch dark and you couldn't see your hand in front of your face. The REM Pod suddenly lit up and it was all four colors which meant it was standing right by it or pretty much touching it. It then got quiet and the footsteps followed and then stopped like twenty feet away. We all got hit with a blast of cold air and I swear I saw a dark figure right in front of us and everyone flipped on their lights and it was gone or at least gone from that location. We turned the lights off again and it was dark once more. This time there were no footsteps, but some loud bangs were heard in certain sections of the basement. Maybe this was the ghost banging stuff into the walls of the one room like we were told. We stayed down there for a little while longer and asked some questions and heard some more knocks and bangs but could not locate the source. There seemed to be some cold spots that would creep up on us after asking some questions, but the hallway was long, and we were uncertain if there were any open windows. We headed down to the other side of the basement but Korin and Kara wanted to go to the attic to see if they could get something while we were downstairs. We let them go and we headed down to where there was an old kitchen. There were some counters in that room we decided to sit on. Kevin and his wife and Travis were next to me. I started again by doing shave and haircut knocking which in return came two knocks right away on the back wall and we clearly heard them. I decided to try it one more time and said thank-you to them for doing it the first time. The second time we heard two knocks again and its been a very long time since anything ghostly has done it for me twice. I was curious if they would do it a third time and I tried it one more time and this time nothing was heard. There was a door to my right that went into a small utility closet and Travis was asking some questions to see who was there when I jumped and Kevin moved just as quick when we heard something take two steps next to us almost like it just walked either out or into that closet and of course nothing that we could see was there. We decided to take a break since we were down there for a while. We headed back upstairs and met with the girls coming down from the attic and they said they saw some shadows moving around in the attic. I said we would switch with them after we take a break.

The long hallways in the basement

We had now switched spots and were in the attic while the girls were in the basement. I turned on the ghost box that runs white noise to communicate with the ghosts. We didn't see any shadow play in the attic but heard some noises come from some of the corners of the attic. We knew there were no animals up here but birds I guess could be up here but didn't see any of them either. I played with the ghost box for a little while and was letting it run and a voice came though it that said girls and danger. Not long after those two words came out of the box, we could hear girls screaming from the floor or floors below and it sounded like Kara and Korin. Sure enough on further review to check on the girls they said while standing in the basement in one of the backrooms and piece of plywood was lifted up into the air and slammed back down right next to them and from there it was scream city. After this experience we needed a break. We headed outside where we found graves on the property.

I stayed back and wanted to eat some more pizza while they did that. I waited for a while, but they were taking a long time, so I headed down one of the hallways by the patient rooms. I felt a little safer as I could just run back to where the pizza room was and not feel like I was stuck in the basement. I walked up to the third floor and listened close and spun around to a noise on the stairs that I had just come up and again it sounded like footsteps. I swear something is following me around this place and it's trying to get me alone. I waited a little longer and felt brave and jumped toward the stairs, but nothing happened so if something was there it was standing it's ground too, and I was not certain I liked that idea. I decided to head back to the pizza room or what we had listed as basecamp. The rest of the team got back from the barn area and the graves but said the only thing they heard was cows mooing in the distance. I said I heard something on the stairs on the third floor again walking toward me.

The stairs on the third floor where I heard footsteps

Kevin, Kara, Korin, Travis, Craig

It was starting to get late and we wanted to visit the basement one more time before calling it a night. We headed down to the basement and went to the far end then around one more corner and sat in the hallway with everyone staggered on the floor a little way away from each other. I set up some motion lights down the hall from us in both directions to see if anything would set them off. I turned on the ghost box and heard a voice come over and say "Danger." It didn't take long for something to follow up that word. The motion lights on the floor all started to light up one right after the other meaning that something was headed our direction of course now we were standing our ground since there is safety in numbers. The lights stopped which meant it was right by us and I said "Get the girls" of course they were not happy I said that and maybe a little freaked out. It was saying some crazy stuff on the device now like "Grab them" and "Get out." Well we were not getting out since we were staying there the rest of the night. It got quiet after that and nothing more was heard so we decided to hit the hay so we could drive home in the morning. I wanted to scare everyone one last time and the owner had showed me where there was a loud buzzer just around a corner in the basement so I snuck in since I was behind everyone and pulled the buzzer which ended with everyone screaming and one person spilling there soda all over them. We had a great time and want to come back for two nights.

CHAPTER 7

FIRST WARD SCHOOL
WISCONSIN RAPIDS, WISCONSIN
By Melissa Clevenger

First Ward School

First Ward School will forever hold a special place in my heart. It is the place where I got my start on the Fox Valley Ghost Hunters team. Savannah and I belonged on a team out of state and we both longed to be on a team close to home that we could be more involved with. One day Savannah saw a post from Fox Valley Ghost Hunters. We decided to be brave and messaged Craig the founder of the team. Craig invited us to spend the weekend with some of the team at First Ward School. At the time neither of us had heard of the school before, but we were beyond excited for a new adventure.

I had to work late that Friday night in March, so Savannah and I didn't arrive at the school until 7 p.m. As Savannah and I got the courage to get out of the car we got to the front door of the school and knocked. Craig was supposed to meet us at the door, so we knew he would come soon. It was about 30 degrees that night, and fifteen minutes later we were still standing at the door. Finally, after freezing to death, we decided to just walk right in. Directly in front of us were stairs and another set of doors that led us to more stairs. We could hear people talking upstairs, so we just made our way up the stairs. Finally, we made it to the room that the team was in and they were all just sitting around a huge table talking. Being frozen to death from waiting outside so long was the ice breaker we needed.

Savannah and I were introduced to the team members that were there that night, and the owner of First Ward School, who also resides there, Justin Libigs. Justin was more than happy to give the two of us an extensive tour of the school and tell us stories. Every inch of the school was thoughtfully decorated with the most amazing pieces of history that I have ever seen. Little did we know that this night would be the first of many adventures for Savannah and me as investigators for the Fox Valley Ghost Hunters.

The History of First Ward School

In the late 1800s, schools began to become overcrowded in Wisconsin Rapids. They decided to build a new state-of-the-art school. This school would be like no other in the area. The school would be heated by coal and equipped with electricity. All the latest technology would be used in the school including blackboards, adjustable seats, and venetian blinds.

The bricks for the 17,000 square-foot building would be made on site. There were four large classrooms in the school that were painted by watercolor. The school was complete in 1896 and would be used to teach grades Kindergarten through the sixth grade. Originally named Irving School in 1902 after the author, Washington Irving. In 1910, the large bell tower on the top of the building was struck by lightning, due to the cost it was never replaced.

FVGH donated to the school and got a brick

As the number of students increased through the years, the school was forced to be only used for students up to the third grade. The teachers were nuns, and they lived in the attic of the school. The nuns began encountering strange things at the school and were said to have kept a log of the activity that occurred, however a log to this day has not been found.

In 1979, the building was abandoned and later bought by the Libigs family in December 2010. Justin lives in the school, along with his spiritual occupants Betty, Oscar, Miss Holliday, Mike, and perhaps many others that still occupy the space with him.

The story of Oscar is that he was a young special needs boy. Due to his disabilities he was often ridiculed and bullied. One day, Oscar was found hanging in the attic. It is not known if Oscar gave into all the bullying and committed suicide or did the bullies themselves hang him. There were no documents of this case, but in those days, suicide was not talked about, and if the children did this to him, they were most likely the children of prestigious families.

Betty was only a young child when she was waiting for the bus when a car got to close to her and caught her dress dragging her down the road. Miss Holliday also makes many appearances at the school to this day. And Mike, the janitor and maintenance guy who had his shop in the basement of the school. These are the spirits who are witnessed most often at the school by Justin and others.

Justin thinks of the spirits who occupy his home as roommates, except they never eat his food. Disembodied voices are often heard throughout the building, footsteps, objects moving, and shadows and apparitions are often seen. Justin believes in being respectful of those who have passed before us, and to treat them as if they were still here.

The kindergarten room in the school

The Investigation of First Ward School

Being the first night that Savannah and I met the team we really didn't know what to expect from the investigation. We were eager to see how the team would investigate and what equipment they had. At this time Savannah and I only had our voice recorders, so we would have to rely on that for what evidence we would get. During the investigation the two of us kept quiet and let Craig conduct the investigation for the night and ask the questions.

The group of us began in the basement where it has been said that a portal may exist in the wall. Each of us took a seat in a small room that had Halloween decorations all around including an actual coffin. We had several good responses with the ghost box and when we asked if Mike was there with us, the REM Pod began to go off instantly. It's been said that Mike doesn't really like women in his space in the basement, so possibly he was checking out the new girls that were inhibiting his space. I could feel the energy in the room as it got stronger and I knew we were not alone in the room. Just then Kara said that something had just grabbed her arm. Several touches and responses later, we decided to continue our investigation in the attic.

We finally made it up all the flights of stairs to the attic. The air was so freezing that every breath we took could be seen like a cloud in the air. Our teeth chattered as we tried to make small talk with each other. Every noise we heard we had to determine if it was a ghost or our legs shaking and hitting the table next to us. Before we ran back downstairs due to the cold, we suddenly heard footsteps coming toward us. Step-by-step I could hear the wooden floorboards creak closer and closer. Then when it was almost directly in front of me it stopped. Complete silence, not a single sound. We sat a little longer in complete silence and still nothing.

By the time we made it back to the bedrooms most of the group was tired and ready for bed. Savannah brought a cot to sleep on and I had an air mattress. I forgot to bring an air pump, so I borrowed one from one of the girls in the group and gave it back to her. We made our beds and got ready for bed. I decided that I would turn my voice recorder on for the night. Being in a new place I didn't know what I may catch on the recorder.

After about an hour of sleeping I could feel my air mattress slowly sinking closer and closer to the ground below me. A few hours later I was flat on the hard floor, but I was able to still fall back to sleep. Suddenly in the darkness I was awaken by my voice recorder flying over my head. It landed with a bang on the ground right in front of my face. Now I honestly didn't think much of the situation, I was just going to pick up my recorder to turn it off. My hand reached to grab my recorder and right as my hand connected with the recorder a male's voice loudly said "Hi" from right behind me. I quickly flipped over only to see that no one was around.

I rolled back over and laid there a few minutes when I decided that I should check the time on my phone so I could tell the others when they woke up. By this time my body ached from sleeping on the hard, bare floor all night. Reaching forward for my phone, my hand landed on something that wasn't my phone. When I realized that my hand landed on an air pump that same male's voice from behind me said "Hello." This voice was not quiet at all, he wanted me to hear him. The odd thing about the air pump was I didn't have an air pump with me, but I sure did need one. I reached for my phone to shine it on the man behind me, but still nothing no one was there. The time was 6 a.m., and the room was still full of darkness.

The next morning, I told Justin everything that happened that night. He stood there patiently listening to my story with a grin on his face the whole time. I wondered if he was grinning because maybe he didn't believe my story. At the end of my story Justin simply smiled and said that doesn't surprise me at all. According to Justin, Mike who was the maintenance guy and caretaker, was probably curious on who the new girl was in the school, and he does not like to be recorded. In fact, Justin said that in the last few months other people who visited the school also told stories of their voice recorders being thrown.

An antique when chair welcomes guests into the school

On another night at First Ward School a few members of the team were investigating in the Coal Room in the basement. I was standing up holding my Mel Meter with REM, and Travis was kneeling below my hand. Suddenly, I felt a warm hand grasp my hand pinching my finger in the stand of the Mel Meter. Before I could even get the words out of my mouth, Travis asked if I just pushed down hard on his head. I said "No, did you just grab my hand really hard?" At the exact moment that my hand was grabbed, something had pushed down on Travis' head directly below my hand. I was puzzled that the hand that grasped me felt so warm and so human.

The First Ward School continues to be one of my favorite places to go. As a team we try to go there as often as we can to visit

Justin and the other spiritual guests that inhabit his home. Justin is one of the sincerest people that I know, and the way that he treats the ghosts in his house as humans is amazing. I am sure we will have many more stories to come, and I cannot wait for our next adventure.

Melissa, Craig, Kara, and Justin at First Ward

CHAPTER 8

Barclay Cemetery Michigan

By Melissa Clevenger

A view of the Barclay Cemetery

Shortly after joining Fox Valley Ghost Hunters I had the opportunity to go to Summerwind, which is a well-known haunted location that the team has regular access to. During my first trip, Craig took us in the daytime to see Barclay Cemetery. Literally in the middle of the woods sat this small fenced in cemetery with perfect little white crosses with flowers around them marking each gravesite. In the center of the crosses was a large sign with the name of each innocent soul that rested on that site. I began reading off each name, what they died from, and finally their age. Soon realizing this was a cemetery that only housed small children.

What I felt when I realized that only children were laid to rest here is very hard to describe. Overall, the cemetery gave off a feeling of peace. I am not sure if it was just the combination of pure Michigan air and the fact that we were in the middle of the woods, but I truly felt peace and calmness. Then came the feeling of mourning for each child who lost their lives so young, and the sorrow that their parents must have felt. Then there are the questions, why were these children not buried with their families, why only children here? These questions, unfortunately I do not know the answers to.

Barclay Cemetery began to be a regular day time stop for us when we went to Summerwind. The more we talked about the cemetery though, the more we wanted to investigate it at night to try and connect with the souls buried there. One weekend we happened to have a free night and decided we would finally give an investigation a shot, what follows was not what we had expected.

The History of Barclay Cemetery

I would like to keep the exact location of the Barclay Cemetery undisclosed because it is important to protect the cemetery and those who rest there. I will tell you it is in the middle of the woods in Michigan. The first child was buried at the cemetery in 1898 and only six short years later in 1904 the last child was buried there. I do not know exactly why the parents chose to bury the children separate from their loving families, and that we may never know.

A sign sits at the cemetery listing the name, age, and cause of death for each child buried there.

Baby Anderson, age 0, cause of death: Born Dead
Paul Anderson, age 3, cause of death: Diptheria
Leander Brisette, age 13, cause of death: Pneumonia
Clyde Bruette, age 8 days, cause of death: Pneumonia
Robert Bruette, age 2, cause of death: Mumps
Rose Jane Bruette, age 19, cause of death:
Consumption
Gilbert Loyd Daniels, age unknown, cause of
death: Typhoid Fever
Lucile Daniels, age 2, cause of death: Measles
Unamed McLeoud, age 2 months, cause of death:
Unknown
Lydia Caroline Sexton, age 3 months, cause of
death: Pneumonia
William Sexton, age 11, cause of death: Consumption
Frank Eisner, age young man, cause of death: Diptheria
Josephine Eisner, age 6, cause of death: Diptheria

My heart goes out to each one of these thirteen beautiful souls. I can only imagine what their families went through. So much heartache and pain. May each angel rest in peace.

The Investigation of Barclay Cemetery

Investigating Barclay Cemetery at night was not in our original plans. We had a pretty busy agenda for the entire weekend. On this Saturday night, we had just finished speaking for an event, and we headed back to our hotel room. This trip was Savannah's first time in the area, so we were excited to tell her all the haunted places that we have investigated around here. Then we began talking about Barclay Cemetery. I told Savannah how we had only been to Barclay during the daylight hours and how peaceful and calm it was there with the children. This was the point where we all decided it would be a great idea to investigate the cemetery at night to see if we could communicate with the spirits of the children.

For this investigation Craig, Travis, Kara, Savannah, and I decided we didn't need very much equipment. We had full intentions of being respectful, so we kept everything to a minimum. I grabbed my Tascam voice recorder and my SB-7 ghost box and the five of us were headed off to the car.

Almost instantly when the car started, I began to feel uneasy. My uneasiness grew more and more as the car accelerated. Once we got closer to the woods and made the right hand turn to our final destination, I began to feel dread.

It was hard for me to explain the dread I felt because Barclay Cemetery was a place that I had always loved going to. I decided to start recording the road in front of us with my phone because I just knew something was in the woods, I could feel it.

In the distance I could see the cemetery on the right-hand side of the road, with woods all around it, simply divided by a road. One by one we got out of the car to begin our investigation. Since it was Savannah's first time here, we began by reading the sign stating each child buried in the cemetery, their age and what they died from. It is always so sad to read how these innocent children passed away.

Craig began asking some basic questions trying to contact the children. I stood facing away from the cemetery staring straight across the street into the woods. What was over there? I could feel it, and I could not take my attention off it, whatever it was. For the first time doing an investigation I felt fear. Fear of the unknown, for some reason whatever it was did not feel like the ghost we were used to communicating with. I was so focused on what I felt across the road in the woods that I was even paying attention to the questions that Craig was asking.

Travis decided to do a ghost box session to see if we could get some immediate responses to the questions we were asking, and to our surprise, we began getting intelligent responses to what we asked. The fear and dread were still there though. All of us felt it, we didn't know what it was, but we knew it wasn't good.

I brought everyone's attention to across the road as we just stood there starring into the woods. The presence was so strong, it was as if an entity was lurking across the street watching our every move. Suddenly Craig saw a black shadow figure walk out of the woods and cross the road directly by where we were standing. It had been watching us all along, but what was it? It was not one of the children buried in the cemetery, so why was it there?

The graves of the children marked by white crosses

Fear began to take over each one of us as we felt the black shadow figure come closer and closer. Then at the brink of our fear, we hear trees rustling in the woods. Something was coming toward us! As we began to head toward where the trees were rustling to investigate, Travis states that it could likely be a Mountain Lion, which is the point that we all bolted toward the car. Many members of our team will bravely walk toward what may be a ghost, but wild animals that could be dangerous was our cutoff point that night.

Safely in the car the feeling of being watched was still there, each one of us felt it now. This was not our typical ghost that we encounter. Travis began driving back to our hotel and I just knew we were being followed. As our hearts raced, we couldn't wait to get back to our hotel room.

Finally, we made it to the end of the road and stopped at the stop sign. Just then I felt an extra presence in the vehicle. The air was heavy, and the car went silent. Kara was the first to be touched in the car. Something kept grabbing her shoulder as we drove and touching her head. Moments later it grabbed Savannah's legs down toward her ankles. Then Craig began to be touched as well. This went on the entire car ride back to our hotel. We knew that we were going to have to listen to our voice recorder right away so maybe we could get an answer to what was following us.

The instant we got back to our hotel room I pulled out my laptop to begin going over audio. Suddenly out of the laptop came a loud robotic voice talking to us. It caught us all by surprise and was rather creepy sounding, but we had no idea what it was saying to us. What we did know was that whatever followed us from the Barclay Cemetery now resided in our hotel room with us.

As the three of us girls sat together on one bed we began listening to our audio from that night. We already knew that we had intelligent answers when the ghost box was used. What we didn't know was every question that we asked prior to the ghost box had answers. We were only at the cemetery for a very short time, maybe thirty minutes, and in that time we had at least fifteen good EVPS answering our questions. As my legs hung over the side of the bed, both of my ankles were grabbed tightly and tugged downward. Startled I quickly pulled my legs up by me in the bed.

That night whatever followed us back wanted its presence to be known. Once we turned the lights off and began to fall asleep things began falling in our room. I could hear someone walking around by the bathroom, yet everyone was in bed. Kara was startled when she was half asleep by a shadow figure staring straight into her face. Savannah felt something touching her leg throughout the night. In the wee hours of the night we all fell asleep to the sounds of crashes and voices coming from directly in our room.

We may never know what watched us that night in the woods and followed us like prey. Although we were scared that night, each one of us eagerly await our chance to go back to Barclay Cemetery. Now we seek answers. We know a presence is there that is not part of the cemetery, but the feeling of it lurking at us and watching our every move intrigues us. What answers may we find on our next journey to Barclay and will the shadow figure still be there waiting in the woods for our next investigation.

CHAPTER 9

GATEWAY LODGE
LAND O' LAKES, WISCONSIN

By Craig Nehring

Gateway Lodge

I spent most of my life a little over an hour away in Minocqua from this amazing lodge. Summerwind is only fifteen minutes from here as well. I got a call from Lola asking if we wanted to do some seminars for their yearly Zombie walk and of course I was more than thrilled at the idea and even better the lodge offered us free rooms while we stayed there since we were doing the seminars from there. When we arrived, we were told we would have access to the haunted rooms and most of the lodge to investigate after the events in the evening. We made our way to the rooms which were very cozy. I decided to look of the history of the lodge before we started our first seminar covering Summerwind in the lobby.

The History of Gateway Lodge

The Gateway Lodge was built by radio and theater magnate John King of Detroit, Michigan. King initially considered Watersmeet, Michigan and Phelps Wisconsin as sites for the complex, but ultimately chose the town of Land O' Lakes, located in Vilas County, Wisconsin. Groundbreaking for the Gateway Lodge began in 1937. The airport was completed in 1938. The original complex consisted of the main lodge. The airport would eventually be located to the south, behind the lodge.

The original cost to build the Gateway Lodge was $100,000. The going rate for a tradesman's labor was 37 cents per hour. The main lodge was originally a one-story structure with approximately sixty-five guest rooms. Some had private baths, but most rooms shared hallway baths.

All the beams were hand-hewn timbers and given a burnt-brown finish. This finish was achieved by applying red-hot irons to the surface of the beam, removing the charred wood, and then coating the surface with varnish. The paneling was made of native pine pieced together in the traditional tongue and groove manner. The beauty of this local craftsmanship is still awe-inspiring and welcomes today's guests with its exemplary artistry.

On the exterior of the lodge, neon lighting was installed under the building's eaves and around the gables. The entire structure simply glowed at night. This feature still functions today and creates that same striking appearance in the dark of the great Northwoods.

The Stan Kellar Trio took over the entertainment from 1946 to 1949. Through King's affiliations in the entertainment industry, he brought many well-known figures to stay and play at the lodge, including Bob Hope, Lawrence Welk, movie star Mitzi Gaynor, and the comedy team of Bud Abbot & Lou Costello.

After King died on January 2, 1952, his family continued to operate the Gateway Lodge complex in its originally constructed format until 1961.

Mr. Walter Williamson purchased the Gateway Lodge on February 17, 1961. He added a second floor and reconfigured the rooms on the first floor. Williamson also built a swimming pool with an overhead glass and beam atrium and a redwood sauna.

Williamson sold the Gateway Lodge to Mr. Degayner in the early 70s. Unfortunately, Degayner could not really afford the property, and he lost it after only one year.

In October of 1989, the bank sold the Gateway Lodge to Robert and Diane Yarbrough from Valentine, Nebraska. They acted as developers to convert the Lodge to a condominium form of ownership.

The Gateway Lounge is now operated by the association management.

Reports of hauntings from the lodge from bar tenders and others include singing in the hallways when no one is there. Some have seen people in period clothing in the halls only to see them disappear. Certain rooms in the lodge are haunted and the staff know what rooms have activity. Some say while in the basement they have heard footsteps come from above, but no one is there when they go up to check.

The Investigation of the Gateway Lodge

We finished the seminar at the lodge in the main area by the fireplace and we had over hundred guests that came to hear about

Summerwind and meet us. It was a cold evening and the fireplace was lit to keep us and the guests warm. We had to wait about an hour for everyone to clear out before we could start. Investigating are Kara, Lynzi, and me. Everyone got cleared out and we were ready to go. The staff gave us keys to three haunted rooms, so we headed to those rooms first. The rooms were on the second floor and two of them were next to each other. We went into the first room. There was the main room with the bed and a couch and off the bedroom was a bathroom and one corner had a small kitchen but a full-size fridge and stove with a kitchen table. I sat at the table with chairs while Lynzi and Kara sat on the bed. I started by asking questions if anyone was in the room. There were a few small knocks from within the room but nothing too exciting. I had a REM Pod on the floor, and I noticed that a shadow moved from the doorway toward the bed the woman was sitting on. The REM Pod went off and lit up all four colors to show it was right there. I told them that I think it was going to be getting on the bed with them and indeed it did. Kara said that something touched her hair and was caressing it and Lynzi felt something on the bed and the mattress moved like there was weight of an unseen object sitting there. I got up and moved the Pod onto the bed and within seconds it was going off to let us know something was spending time on the bed with them. I turned the ghost box on to ask questions so they can talk to us in real time. When I asked who was on the bed a voice came back and said "I am." I asked who it was but there was no reply and the next thing out of the box was a voice saying it was touching them. Kara said something touched her leg. The REM Pod went off one more time and then it was quiet. I however heard one of the kitchen chairs that was right across from me move and slide on the floor. I jumped a little since it was pitch dark and did not expect it. I thought maybe our ghostly friend got up from the bed and now joined me at the kitchen table. We heard nothing more, so we decided to try another room.

The next room was right next to the one we were just in and we attempted to try the same thing but other than a few noises all was quiet. We decided to take a trip to the attic to see what was up there. The attic was at the end of the hall which looked like a room door that was not marked. I opened the door to find some stairs and we climbed the stairs. It was a lot warmer than I expected and figured someone did a good job insulating. There was a bunch of stuff stored up here for different seasons and festivities. We investigated for a short time up here but nothing out of the ordinary was happening, so we headed back downstairs.

Our next spot to investigate was the basement so we headed down the steps and there was one large room with a couch possible a breakroom for the employees. There was a hallway heading back off the room that we walked down, and it went quite a way. We checked to see where every door led, and one went under the building like a crawl space but enough room to stand in there. It was all sand and I figured we could stop back and check it out, but I wanted to continue down the hall to see where it led. At the end of that hall was another hall that went down just as far but I could see the end to that one. We walked down that hall past some coolers and storage areas to almost the end where one entrance went into a laundry room with some commercial machines and where all the towels were stored for the guests. The other side had a staircase that went back upstairs and where the power was at coming into the building. It was not the easiest to investigate down here with all the noises coming from the machines, so I suggested we try under the building where we saw all the sand. We wandered inside underneath the building and there was a wooden plank going over a hole that had water down below. There was a moment that I felt like I was walking a plank to get to the other side and thought I wander what is in that water below or how deep it is. Kara and Lynzi were a little apprehensive about walking the plank because it weren't that stable and if one end let loose down you would go. They both made it and now we were standing in the sand under the lodge. It was cold underneath there and we did not stay long. I snapped some pictures and one had a weird mist and it was farther away from us, so it was not our breath. I did not think too much of it since it was cold, but it was just an odd picture. Well the cold was starting to get to me, so we decided to head back up by the fireplace to warm up.

Now back upstairs sitting by the fire and we were tired, and the heat was putting us to sleep so we decided to call it a night. I had my own room and the girls had one too. Some of us would not be getting much sleep though.

The Gateway Lodge main area

I awoke next morning to Kara and Lynzi telling me about their night in the room. Kara woke up in the middle of the night and saw a shadow standing next to Lynzi by her bed. When she had talked to her about it Lynzi said she had seen it too. It did not do anything but just stand there. Maybe that was the same shadow we saw in the other room that was on the bed with them. We had one more night there and went back and investigated the same rooms but this time it was Saturday evening and more guests were there so it was hard to investigate because you didn't know where the noises were really coming from. We called it an early night and it was a quiet one.

We want to thank Gateway Lodge and Lola for the fun evening and access to some haunted rooms. This an amazing place close to many other haunted locations like Summerwind and the Paulding light in Michigan. We look forward to visiting the area and staying here again.

One of the rooms in Gateway Lodge

Savannah, Melissa, Kara at the Gateway Lodge 2019

CHAPTER 10

DEVIL'S PUNCHBOWL
MENOMONIE, WISCONSIN
By Melissa Clevenger

Devil's Punchbowl

We were brought to Menomonie to speak at a conference at the Mabel Tainter. Craig, Travis, and I got to stand on the stage and tell stories of the haunted locations that we have had the opportunity to investigate. This was my first time to speak in front of a large crowd. I was nervous leading up to the moment, but once we started, I was completely comfortable because we are so passionate about what we do.

Grant Wilson from Ghost Hunters was the headliner for the weekend. Grant is somebody who I have always highly respected, so I was overly excited for the opportunity to meet him. Craig had a table for the weekend to sell his products, and Savannah and I had a table for the products that we make. Our weekend became even better when Grant decided to have his table next to ours for the weekend. We all had the opportunity to hang out with Grant and talk to him all weekend. He really is an amazing asset to the paranormal field.

Once the conference was over it was time to pack up our stuff and head home. For a paranormal team, no trip is complete without some investigating though. Craig began to tell us about a location called The Devil's Punchbowl that was on our way home. As a team we are used to investigating haunted locations and of course ghosts. This location, however, was not our usual investigation. Devil's Punchbowl is known for stories of mythical creatures. The thought of investigating stories of gnomes and fairies was intriguing to all of us. And so, our journey to the Devil's Punchbowl began.

Where the gnomes like to play

CRAIG NEHRING AND MELISSA CLEVENGER

The History of The Devil's Punchbowl

Stories of gnomes, trolls, and fairies are nothing new to society although very few people can ever say that they have ever seen one. Often referred to as Nature Spirits or Elementals, their stories have been passed on through fairy tales or legends. One such location with stories of sightings of gnomes, trolls, and fairies is from the Devil's Punchbowl. Originally known as Black's Ravine by a Captain from the Civil War who owned the land. Many believe the area carries the name of the Devil's Punchbowl from the University of Wisconsin's mascot the Blue Devil.

The Devil's Punchbowl which was formed from post glacial flooding, is a beautiful place to go hiking or birdwatching, but birds may not be all that you witness. One story tells of an officer who walked down the steps to the bottom of the punchbowl, upon looking up to the top of the cliffs he sees a row of what looked like tiny men peering down at him. He quickly looked away thinking he was seeing things, but when he looked back up, they were still there. Through the years, others have told stories of seeing these little men up in the trees, or fairies fly by. There have been many reports of people seeing gnomes and trolls run through the punchbowl and the tunnel.

It is recommended if you are visiting the punchbowl you should bring Skittles or shiny objects to leave for the trolls. Supposedly, visitors who fail to leave gifts often return to their cars to find that they will not start. It has been said that if you take water from the bowl it will remain cold for days even during the summer months. It is a beautiful place even if you do not see what is hidden from your eyes.

The Investigation of the Devil's Punchbowl

We really did not know what to expect coming into this investigation considering we are used to investigating ghosts. During the drive Craig told us stories that he had heard though the years from the Devil's Punchbowl. Trolls, gnomes, fairies, how in the world do we investigate this? We have ghost hunting equipment, does ghost hunting equipment even work for mythical creatures? This defiantly was not what we were used to investigating, but in the end, we decided to keep it simple. We decided for this investigation we would only use a voice recorder and a camera. Sometimes it is best to just be in the moment and pay attention to everything around you. This was one of those moments, not all investigations require tuns of equipment.

The first thing we look at is the tunnel where some have seen trolls run through. I know none of us expected to see a troll in the tunnel, but we couldn't help but hope. Seeing a ghost is normal to me, I am not so sure how I would react to a troll. Today we did not see a troll in the tunnel. To get to the bottom of the punchbowl would require walking down several flights of stairs. As we walked step-by-step surrounded by the woods, we could hear a waterfall.

Finally, we made it to the bottom of the stairway and into the punchbowl. I stood there in awe taking in the scenery that surrounded us. This place was absolutely magical, there is no other word to describe it. In front of us was the most breathtaking waterfall surrounded by trees all around the top of the bowl. It was now time for the adventure to begin.

I must admit that when I first scanned the cliff above me, I really did expect to see a gnome peering down. Each of us stood there looking back and forth in hopes of seeing what could be hidden up in the trees above us. No gnomes in sight, but what I can say is that even the air felt magical. It felt like something could happen at any moment. At this point Mike noticed the leave on the ground in front of him. We couldn't help but notice that this particular leaf had the perfect smiling face on it. As we were admiring the perfect smiling leaf, suddenly there was the snapping of several sticks behind us. We all spun around hoping to see something behind us. Nothing but the entrancing waterfall to be seen.

The smiling leaf

As we began to walk around, I noticed leaves compressing down, but I did not see anything around. We started studying the ground around us and noticed other leaves moving around. There were some chipmunks running around, so it was highly likely that they were moving the leaves around, but in the moment, we couldn't help but think just maybe it was something mythical.

The final story that we were told was about leaving Skittles or shiny objects for the trolls to appease them. Well, it was no surprise that me being the candy lover that I am, I just happened to have a bag of Skittles with me for the ride. I do love my candy, but I was willing to spare some candy to keep the trolls happy.

The Devil's Punchbowl is an enchanting place to walk around and enjoy nature. Even though we never saw gnomes, trolls, or fairies we still can imagine that they exist. It is possible that this location is better to be experienced alone or in a small group. I do believe that if you are meant to see these creatures then you will. On this particular day, we were not meant to see them, and I was ok with that. Who knows what the next trip here will entail?

CHAPTER 11

Summerwind Round 50
Land O' Lakes, Wisconsin

By Craig Nehring

Summerwind the 80s

Summerwind is known around the world for being one of the most haunted places in the world and its in almost every haunted book you pick up in Wisconsin and on numerous web sites claiming the same thing. I called this round 50 because that is a rough estimate how many times, we have investigated this amazing place. Let me note that this is private property and our team has sole permission to investigate when we so desire which is like every year.

I am honored in so many ways to have been close to the owners and family though the years. They are an amazing couple who's love for the property is shared with many. We have been working though the years to find someone to back a project of rebuilding the notorious haunted house with the original blueprints into a museum. In that museum would be many artifacts from the house including some original shutters that sit in my garage that came off the place prior to the fire. We have gotten close sometimes to finding that person with some producers that wanted to fund the project but not finding the network to pull the plug. How fascinating would it be to see the mansion rebuilt ghosts and all and be able to say look what we just did. Maybe that person is out there still and will jump at the idea of a haunted house built with the original blueprints from Tallmadge and Watson. The love of Summerwind has been shared with many of my teammates new and old along with many friends over the years. I dedicate this article to a close friend, who loved Summerwind as much as me, Kevin Malek who passed away unexpectedly this past year. We both would investigate this property with our equipment and come away with amazing stories to tell. We both cared for the property and we cleaned it up every year from all the people that would trespass and toss their garbage everywhere. First and foremost, there is the amazing history.

The History of Lilac Hills aka Summerwind
In 1914 a Lodge was constructed on West Bay lake called Lilac Hills and it was a fishing lodge for families to come in off the lake and

relax. I happened to come across an article for the lodge and the cost of five dollars to stay the night. There were very few trees and the lodge sat high above the water on the hill. Surrounding the lodge were lilac bushes which gave the name to the place. The name Summerwind would not even be heard of till the 70s but that is another story you will find later in this chapter.

Robert Lamont

In 1916 it was first a fishing lodge that was then bought and reno-vated by Robert Patterson Lamont in 1916. The renovations took two years. Robert was U.S. Secretary of Commerce under Hover who had supposedly been rumored to have stayed in the mansion. The house was used as a vacation home for Lamont and his family. Over the next fifteen years, the family experienced haunting's inside the walls of the seemingly peaceful retreat. It was long after moving in that the Lamont's began to share with friends and neighbors their ghost stories of objects that moved by themselves, strange noises echoing from seemingly empty rooms and shadows that went from room to room. While the family found these occurrences strange, they were never enough to stop the Lamont's from visiting the house, that was, until one evening while sitting down for dinner a dark shadow made it way though the foyer doors. Robert pulled out his black powder pistol and fired three shots missing the dark mass as the bullets went right though it and lodged into a door on the other side. Those bullet holes would remain in the door till the fire engulfed the mansion in 1988. Robert and his family fled never to return.

After sitting empty for years, it was sold in the 1940s to the Keefer family who also used the house as a vacation home, renting the large property out to visitors. Many passing tenants claimed Mrs. Keefer rarely set foot inside the house, often handing the keys to guests. In the 70s the house again was sold, and more hauntings would continue.

Arnold and Ginger Hinshaw would be the new owners and their six kids. Things didn't take long to manifest for them to realize that the mansion was haunted. Lights would turn on and go off and dark shadows would move down the hallways. Contractors that were to come and remodel would not show up due to the reputation of the house being haunted. Tools would go missing and when measuring a room, the dimensions of that room would change in size the next day. Windows would open and close and they had to nail them shut from the inside. A car once started on fire for no apparent reason and whispered voices came from the darkness. Things would get much worse as the family came across a small crawlspace behind a dresser. They sent one of their young daughters April inside to look. She came out screaming that there was a corpse inside the wall with black matted hair still hanging off the skull. However, this was never reported to the police for some reason and later when they returned the corpse had vanished.

Ginger and her children said they felt as though they were being watched by something and strange noises could be heard coming from rooms but on investigation, they would find nothing there. Ginger while in the kitchen was visited by a lady in white and this is especially important because this will also appear later in the story of Summerwind. Arnold started playing a Hammond organ late into the night stating that the ghosts told him to play or they would be upset. With everything going on the family was overtaken by stress and sadness and Ginger contemplated suicide. Ginger and the children finally had enough and moved out just six months after living in their dream home. Arnold finally left as well leaving this very haunted place abandoned once more. I did some studies on the family for a long time and located one of the members not that long ago. Many of things that happened to this family were not all that accurate and many of the things I just wrote became exaggerated and not true. I however included them because it was known to have taken place and in all the books. The corpse is what I find hard to believe since why would one not call the police in that instance of finding a body? In further interviews I come to find out the corpse was also a fable that made a family very well known.

Raymond Bober, Ginger's father, decided he would purchase the property and turn it into a restaurant and inn. However, during the construction of the restaurant, Ginger's brother reportedly saw an apparition on the second floor and, upon running down to the first floor saw the same ghost in white. He also heard gun shots and smelled gun powder, but nothing was found. Raymond while sleeping one night had a dream of an explorer named Jonathon Carver who told him that he had a deed with the Native Americans to 1/3 of Northern Wisconsin and it was buried in the foundation of Summerwind. He told Raymond he needed to find that deed so he could be set free. Again, I did some digging. Jonathon Carver had never made it that far north in his explorations to be able to put a deed into the foundation. There was never anything that any of the construction workers buried into the foundation and the real deed was found in a museum in England as I was able to document. Raymond dreams kept him up at night and soon he had enough as well and left the property vacant again. He wrote a book called the Carver Effect under pen name Wolfgang Von Bober. The book is extremely hard to find and most that were checked out were never returned. I have one in my possession and many of the things listed in that book are also extremely hard to fathom. I believe some of what happened to be true but in my opinion it's a great way to sell books at the time in the 70s from a house very well known for its hauntings.

A little piece of the puzzle Raymond Von Bober one morning while taking a walk came across a sign that was laying in the road covered with dirt. On that sign was some carved-out letters that said Summerwind. Now the new name for the mansion was called Summerwind.

In 1986, this amazing lady said to her husband I would like something different for my anniversary. Her husband came back with the deed to Summerwind. This amazing couple is how I found this amazing haunted location although I heard rumors of it while I was going to school in Minocqua. I wouldn't know who owned it till many years later. The mansion was not much to look at since vandals and kids would use it as a party spot to try to see ghosts. It didn't help much that *Time Life Magazine* listed it as one of the top nine haunted houses in the United States. Now people flocked from miles around to get a glimpse of this house or what was left of it. The owners wanted to make it into a bed and breakfast, but the house was in such bad shape that funds were not available. I will tell more of their stories later since I didn't know them quite yet.

I was in Lakeland Union High School at the time from 85 to 88 ironically with fellow friend and investigator of his own future team Kevin Malek. Everyone knew about Summerwind and it was a weekly routine to go visit the place and while the parties still took place the hauntings were active as well. We would see shadows that we could not explain and hear voices. Lights would come on in rooms but there was no electricity at all in the house. The early 80s I heard people that visited would drive there and not be able to leave because their car would not start. Faces and odd anomalies would appear in people's pictures. I had been there plenty of times and for most of us later in the 80s it got old, so we didn't go there that often anymore. My dad was starter out at Trout Lake Golf Course, and he knew one of the neighbors to Summerwind who would talk about the mansion from time to time. One day in 1988 he came home and said that the guy that lived next to the house said that it was stuck by lightning on Father's Day and burned to the ground. I couldn't believe it and was sad that this incredibly famous haunted place was now gone well kind of.

In 2011 I did some digging to find the current owners and it wasn't easy. It was the same owners since 1986 who purchased it as an anniversary present. Their dreams were shot down with the Fire on Father's Day in 88. They had so many amazing stories to tell and said our team could have sole access for doing tours and events up there for the public. They said that one time they stayed in a trailer on the property since the house was unlivable. They decided to walk up and see the house because there was a full moon. As they got closer the house was moving in the moonlight. It looked as though it was breathing in and breathing out as though it was alive. They were startled at this notion. She said I should get hold of the lady that lives on the island because she has some amazing stories about Summerwind but she was in her 90s and she wasn't sure if she was still alive. I was able to locate her and to my surprise she was alive and kicking. There are two main stories to what she had to say which brings back the lady in white again. The first one talks about when she was a young girl maybe twelve years old. A friend and her were out fishing on West Bay lake in front of the mansion when a violent storm hit out of nowhere. They were scared but saw a woman with long black hair in a white dress waiving them to come ashore. They thought the boat would sink so they rowed to where the woman was at and they got out of the boat and the women waved at them to follow her. They walked up the hill to the mansion and she asked them to come inside out of the rain. They went inside and sat on the couch. The lady in white walked up the staircase in front of them and disappeared halfway up the stairs. They were so freaked out that they ran out of the mansion and back down to the boat and luckily the storm was now not that bad, so they got back in the boat and went home.

The next day the two girls even though they were terrified were also intrigued and wanted to go back so again they grabbed the boat and headed back to where they saw the lady in white standing. This time however she was waving at them to stay away which made the two girls sad. They thought why she would not want them there. Later in the day they heard the news that a caretaker over at Lilac Hills went mad and was shooting at people. The girls figured the lady in white saved their lives. That was the last time they saw the lady in white. Seeing that the lady in white had long black hair and the corpse that was found in the wall in the 70s that disappeared also had long black hair. I wonder at all if possible, this was the lady in white since she seems to tend to vanish multiples times throughout the stories.

The Investigations of Summerwind

We have investigated Summerwind so many times that round 50 is about correct and though the years have done seminars and hosted events and people always say the same thing. While no one should trespass on this property nor should they walk off with anything that is not theirs like bricks from the foundation not just because it is stealing but also because they say bad luck follows from a girl breaking two legs after removing a brick to a car of a teenager that starts on fire after putting the brick inside her car. These are just some of the horrific things that had happened from taking something from the property, so my suggestion please don't do it.

Some of the more memorable investigations of Summerwind not in any order are as follows. One night while our team was there, we decided to put two team members in isolation up in the woods opposite the mansion. The two girls had a camera on them while the rest of us sat by the fire a couple hundred yards away. We were enjoying the fire when we heard the girls screaming. They said a Raccoon fell out of tree and landed next to them. They were so startled that they had enough. Later when I reviewed the video, I captured a voice that said I pushed it after it had fallen out of the tree. Now that was just a little bit creepy. One weekend we were picked to do the biggest ghost hunt in the world live from Summerwind but unfortunately the Wi-Fi signal would not work for us, so we gave up and decided to just investigate. We had guests there that night and one of the guests captured something amazing as she panned her video camera to the top of the stairs something was there but what was it. I watched the video when I got home and to my astonishment found the lady in white with long black hair standing for a moment and she doesn't just vanish, but she hovers away right out of the screen off the cameras view. Another night of investigations while guests were there Kevin had a SLS camera and was tracking a ghost that was climbing a tree. The SLS camera picks up stick figures and uses Xbox green dots to capture things that we can't see. Kevin and his wife Jennifer that same night also captured a black shadow leaving the basement and heading up the hill and out of sight.

The staircase where the woman in white was seen at the top

One time while in the basement of Summerwind I turned on the ghost box and voice of a little girl comes though and says " Little girl dead is your friend." Every hair on the top of my head stood up and the REM Pod suddenly goes off. I listen back to the recorder and a voice says, "We really like Craig."

Now it's time for a walk into the woods to see if anything can talk to us out in the woods. We made our way down to the waterline which is a feat because it's so steep. We walked around the property and I jumped high as a kite when I see eyes in the dark. It was a deer but freaked us out. Later on, review of audio after I get scared a voice says, "What an asshole." Well at least the ghosts have a sense of humor.

That night the sky was raining rocks that were falling out of the sky like little pebbles landing around us and next to us. One even hit one of our investigators in the nose. I looked up birds that could do this at night and nothing came up. That wasn't the only time that night that it happened. Around 1 in the morning the girls who were on the team woke up to rocks hitting their tent. We came out to make sure they were ok. I used a thermal camera to check the area but could find no one tossing any rocks at their tent. I woke the next morning to Mama bear walking past the tent and I remained still. The girls were scared and said they were holding each other as there was scratching on the bottom of their tent. One investigator got out of her car when I knew she was in a tent. We asked what happened she said that she heard this gosh awful thing screaming in the woods. I said I heard it too and it was a fox.

The front of Summerwind that leads into basement

A shuttering experience to say the least was when we had an event and a guest brought the shutters to Summerwind to give to me. We stuck them in the car of our investigators and headed on out to check the town out that night. On the way back from town something grabbed my leg in the car. I felt fingers, ice-cold fingers on my leg. I jumped and said something grabbed me and I at first thought the person in the front seat reached back and grabbed me. Nope they did not. We got back to Summerwind and we got out except one of the team members that drove stayed inside the car a little longer. She jumped out screaming saying something was in the car with her. She grabbed some sage and said a prayer, but something was in the car, but no one could see it and I assume attached to the shutters. We walked over to the front of the mansion and I turned the ghost box on and asked who was with us and a voice came back and said "Ghosts." They were not lying. I turned it off and walked up to the car where the shutters were to get something out and thought I heard a voice behind me but couldn't make it out. I rewound the recorder to play it back and heard the voice more clearly say "Dammit I'm being bad." Well something was being bad that night to grab my leg and stuff. We have always had tons of fun camping at Summerwind no matter who was with us. Its been an amazing journey and some interesting and dangerous times as well. One of our investigators had to go to the bathroom but rather than going somewhere in the woods decides to mosey on down to the foundation and step up and venture out to the front of the mansion. He lost his footing because all I hear is a loud noise in the debris and trees. Little did we know there was a large spike sticking out of an old timber that his arm caught on and ripped the skin down his arm. There was so much blood that we had to call 911 who met him down at the end of the driveway. He came back after twenty-seven stiches later and stayed the rest of the weekend.

The exploding soda can. Call us crazy or don't call us at all. We are known for sometimes thinking outside the box and that's a bad thing. We had most of our older team together on this outing and I think it was the next night after the injury above that we decided to place a full soda on the fire on a tray used for cooking. It sat there for awhile when we started to notice it getting bigger and bigger. One of the girls on our team walked over and looked at the can to find out what it was we were doing. That was a bad idea as it exploded all over her and the can was like gone like disintegrated. We never found the can and there was some raw video floating around on the internet.

Our newest members finally got to see Summerwind and they love the place as much as everyone else though the years. We have always tried to keep the place clean and while we don't make a mess other that trespass do. We host events up there so people don't go on private property without permission. The current owners who lost the house in 1988 have lots of memories but even as the ruins age so do they. Recently one of the owners had a stroke and Summerwind may be all but a memory in the future. We hope to do more investigations there, but time may not be on our side. We would like to thank the owners for many years of amazing moments. Summerwind was the best anniversary present a husband could give to his wife.

Pictured L-R are Travis, Melissa, Savannah, Craig, and Kara

A look to the lake under the arches

CHAPTER 12

NATIONAL RAILROAD MUSEUM GREENBAY, WISCONSON

By Melissa Clevenger

National Railroad Museum

As a team we were used to investigating old schools, houses, stores, and even cemeteries, a train museum however, was something different for most of us. Before our investigation I would not have thought of trains as being overly exciting. When I was a young child my mom, my brother Eric, and I had taken a train a few times from our home in Kansas to Wisconsin. As a child such a long train ride was quite the adventure, but through the years I seemed to have forgotten about those trips. I knew that sitting on some of the passenger trains would be certain to bring back some of those childhood memories.

Before arriving at the museum, I was a little optimistic about a train museum being haunted. Travis and I drove from Sheboygan to Green Bay to meet Craig and Kara at the museum. When we arrived, it was still light outside and the weather was perfect. Craig met us at the gate to let us into the museum parking lot. We decided to walk around outside while we waited for Kara to arrive. All around the building were a variety of old trains. I was surprised at how excited I was to see these trains. Really anything with history is intriguing to me so I knew tonight would be a good night. As it began to get a little darker out Kara finally pulled up to the gate. Our investigation inside would start soon.

The History of The National Railroad Museum

An interesting thing about the National Railroad Museum is that some of the trains that are inside the building were there before the building was built and they just built around them. The museum was founded in 1956 and in 1958 was recognized as the National Railroad Museum. It has since become one of the largest railroad museums in the nation. The museum is used as an educational experience for the young and old on the history of the railroad industry.

The museum houses some well-known trains such as the Dwight D. Eisenhower locomotive and command cars. The Dwight D. Eisenhower is the only A4 Class locomotive that is in the United States. The train was used during World War II by Eisenhower himself and was his mobile command center.

There is also the Union Pacific #4017 which is known as the Big Boy at 1.1 million pounds it was used to haul heavy freight. The Pennsylvania RR #4890 was originally used to haul passengers. The Pullman tells the story of the men who had worked the railroads for over hundred years and helped shape our nation's history. Each train tells a part of history and what role it played.

The Investigation of The National Railroad Museum

After a short tour of the museum and hearing a few stories about some of the hauntings that occur at the museum, we were ready for lights out. Our investigation was to begin inside the Dwight D. Eisenhower. The four of us walked onto the train and into a meeting room that was used by Eisenhower during World War II. There were chairs all around the outside of the room as if it were ready for a meeting or maybe an investigation. Each of us took a seat uncertain of what the night ahead of us had in store.

Craig began with the ghost box so that we could ask questions and hopefully get immediate answers. The fact that we were inside a train that was inside a cement building very few radio stations came through the ghost box at all. This was nice because the answers that came back to our questions were clear. One of the first questions asked was "Who's train was this?" Upon playback the answer that we received was "Ike First Captain." This was a pretty impressive response since President Eisenhower was often referred to as Ike.

Kara then said who is this and we all immediately heard the response of "Dwight." A natural response for us was "hi," and the man speaking on the ghost box said "hi" right back to us. The responses we were receiving on the ghost box were incredible. After these clear responses, the ghost box went quiet as if Dwight had stepped away. We decided we would take a break from the Eisenhower train to inspect some of the other trains in the museum.

Next the four of us walked onto a red passenger train. The air immediately changed when we walked onboard to a dense heavy feeling. We each took separate seats across from one another as Travis walked around with the video camera. I can't explain exactly how I felt on this passenger train. My feelings were so uneasy, I felt extremely uncomfortable on this train.

As Kara and Craig took turns asking questions the REM Pod began to go off randomly with each question they asked. I sat in my seat shaking my legs and fidgeting I didn't know why I was so uncomfortable; all I knew was that I needed to get off this train. This train was not scary at all, but I did not like the feeling that it gave me. I gave the investigation a few more minutes before I decided to jump up and announce that we should check out the next train.

Kara, Craig, and Melissa by the Eisenhower

Inside of car where Melissa had uneasy feelings

Once we were off the red train, we figured it was a good time for a little break. Kara came through for us on break with a bag full of snacks. She had the best gummy butterfly's ever along with some other great treats. We sat there discussing the many different trains in the museum trying to figure out which one we were going to investigate next. Travis suggested the Palmer which seemed like a good choice to jump onboard next.

As we walked onto the Palmer the air did not feel like the last train we were on. We walked around a little and asked a few questions but didn't feel like much was happening. Craig played back the recording to see if anything was on there. The first thing we heard was a women's voice saying her name was "Alice." What we heard

ARCHIVES OF A GHOST HUNTER II

next was defiantly a surprise. As Craig was explaining the train to us, we could hear on the recording a lady humming loudly the tune of a song. I have no clue what the song is that the lady was humming, but the tone and beat is stuck in my head to this day. It always amazes me what we hear on our recordings that we cannot hear with our own ears.

The rest of our night would be spent investigating the Eisenhower train. We split up into two groups, Travis and I took the front of the train and Craig and Kara decided to investigate the back. Although we were on the same train the experiences that we had as separate groups were completely different.

Travis and I decided to sit on one of the beds in the sleeping quarters. Each room was rather small where we only had room to sit on the bed and we could barely see into the hallway next to us. At first all we could hear was complete silence all around us.

As we sat on that small hard bed, we could hear footsteps coming toward us from the front of the train. Craig and Kara were all the way at the back of the train, so these footsteps were not from them. The steps became louder and louder as they came closer to the room that we were in. When whoever was out there finally came to a rest in front of our door, I stood up to see who was there. As I shined my flashlight in both directions, I quickly realized that we were all alone. Someone who could not be seen was standing in front of the door watching us sitting on the bed.

As I sat back down on the bed, I decided to pretend like a ghost was not standing in the doorway watching us. Suddenly the bed we were sitting on began rocking to where we could even hear the metal legs hitting the hard floor. The rocking got stronger to where Travis and I were swaying back and forth. Next the train car that we were in started to feel like it was actually moving. At this point the shaking was getting intense as I yelled out to Craig and Kara to see if they were experiencing what we were. They yelled back that there was no movement at the back of the train. We continued to sit there as the

95

rocking began to stop and the train went back to the silence that it began with.

Craig and Kara took up their investigation at the back of the Eisenhower train. Kara sat in one of the sleeping rooms on a bed, as Craig stood in the hallway just outside the door. The first ten or fifteen minutes that they spent back there nothing really was happening. They were hopeful that their part of the investigation would become more eventful.

As Kara sat in pure silence on the bed, she could feel the bed beside her compress down as if someone were slowly sitting down next to her. She could feel the energy from whatever was only inches away from her. As Kara was focused on whatever shared her space, Craig suddenly blurted out that something grabbed his arm. As he turned piercing into the darkness behind him, he could see what appeared to be a dark mass. It is hard to imagine something appearing darker than the darkness that already surrounded us.

Craig continued to feel a presence behind him at the very back of the train. At this point Kara joined Craig in the hallway of the train to see if she could feel what Craig was experiencing. As Kara walked farther back on her own, she felt something touch her shoulder and then her head. She quickly swung around and saw the black mass in the hallway. Craig decided he was going to step into one of the rooms just as the door in front of him slammed shut all on its own.

Travis and I decided to join Craig and Kara at the back section of the train to finish our investigation for the night. We could hear footsteps coming from the front of the train again although nobody else was on the train. I stood in the hallway alone as the others each stepped into a different room. I could feel the energy from the presence that Kara and Craig told me about. The feeling that I got was that whatever it was, it did not want us to go any farther to the back of the train. Almost like it was protecting it for some reason. Out of the corner of my eye, I too caught a glimpse of the black mass at the back of the train.

As we went over our audio, we did not have much else come through, but what we experienced was more than we could have ever expected. I have to say that I can now rank trains as one of my favorite investigations. I learned a lot from this trip, and I also learned that Kara brings good snacks to investigations. I now have a new love for trains, and I hope that we get the chance to investigate the National Railroad Museum again.

The Big Boy Train

CHAPTER 13

CAPTAIN'S WALK WINERY
GREEN BAY, WISCONSIN

By Craig Nehring

Captain's Walk Winery

have been able to investigate this place three times and give a seminar here as well. We investigated the sister winery in Algoma, Wisconsin and that is in one of our other books. I have been friends with the owners for a long time and have done all types of different haunted events from these two wineries. The last time we investigated it was a show that hopefully at some point will come out and can be seen by the general public. On this investigation was Celena, Melissa, and me. First we should talk a little about the history.

The History of Captain's Walk and the Haunting's

Captain's Walk is a beautiful example of a historic home with traditional Greek Revival style and Italianate accents. The cupola on top of the house, often called a captain's walk or a widow's walk, is meant to represent a miniature version of the house itself.

Elisha Morrow built the home in 1857 for his wife, a local woman named Josephine Sayre and his six beautiful daughters. The second youngest daughter, Helen Morrow, inherited the home and owned it until 1920. She was forced to sell the house due to financial hardship. Since 2006 there seems to be a ghost lurking around the winery. Helen is seemed to be the one that is haunting the place, still upset that she had to give up her happy home. Most of the employees have seen her over the years. She moves wine glasses and even throw some. She is known for turning lights on and off as well as the radio and water faucets. She even moves the freight elevator up and down. Some have heard her running upstairs and giggling.

The Investigation of Captain's Walk

I arrived at Captain's Walk and I saw Celena and Melissa sitting in their cars waiting to go inside. There were still some guests inside so we were waiting for them to leave so we could take a quick tour since Melissa and Celena had never been there. We walked inside to meet with one of our guides that would stay there with us till we leave. We came in the back entrance which takes you to hallway that crosses to the left with the main bar and one of the tasting rooms. The right side had a smaller bar and a see through floor into the basement where you would see the barrels of wine down there. Upstairs are some more rooms with couches for guests to hang out in and drink or if they host parties. A door upstairs also leads to attic which in turn leads to the cupola where you can see throughout the city. We also headed down to the basement and saw all the barrels. The walks seemed incredibly old with jagged rock sticking out in places. The back of the basement had boxes of wine for shipping out. Well we had the tour down for new people so next question was where we should investigate.

Melissa sitting in the celler by the barrels of wine

Our first stop to investigate was the bar areas. I was using a video camera to film for our show we were working on. We set up a REM Pod on the bar and everyone had voice recorders to pick up any electronic voices that we couldn't hear. We started out by asking questions although it was hard with some traffic out on the road out front. Other than a couple clicks by the bar area it was noticeably quiet. We headed to the basement to see what we could capture down there. We all sat around a table that was at the bottom of the stairs. When I asked if someone was there, I heard a noise, and something moved. There was a compressor that turned on in the back corner and many times when we investigate some places you must deal with the other noises from furnaces in the winter to compressors for coolers and everything else. I played the voice recorder back to see if anything could be heard and sure enough a voice says "Compressor." So, the ghost knew the compressor was on and said it. After those couple noises everything got quiet in the basement.

Our next stop was the second floor. We split up into a couple rooms to see what we could hear. I was asking questions and we heard a noise in the hallway a couple times. Celena thought something had touched her hair while she was sitting on the couch. We continued to hear noises out in the hallway so we decided to sit out in the hallway on the floor to see if it would continue. I did stand closer to the stairs and Celena was on the floor next to me. Melissa was close to the door that led to the attic. We were asking if Helen were with us tonight and the moment, I said Helen one of the stairs creaked in front of me which was odd because they were carpeted but I am sure they could still make noise. Immediately after the creak there was a loud growl and we all jumped back away from the stairs. That was a little unnerving to hear that. We could see nothing on the stairs but there was something there watching us. It was only a short time after that happened that Melissa started complaining about a bad headache and thought she would have to leave. We grabbed her some Aleve to see if that would help and decided to take a break downstairs in hopes her headache would go away.

The stairs where we heard the growl

Our destination next was the cupola at the top of the attic and Melissa's headache was better so we headed up there. The stairs were steep to the point that you were climbing straight up. Once on the first landing that was the attic part where lots of stuff for the holidays were stored. The next set of stairs headed up to where I wanted to be. The last time we investigated here it was a windy night and we couldn't hear a thing. The stairs going up were just as steep and there was a trap door, we had to push up to go into the cupola. Once up we had to wedge something in the trapdoor and keep it closed but not all the way so it didn't lock us in and if we kept it open I was worried about us falling through the opening in the dark. It only took a couple minutes for me to ask if anything followed us up to when the REM Pod lit up in all the colors to tell us something now was up there with us. There was no where out of there except down and whatever was there with us was in arm's length. We still saw nothing, and I decided I was going to try my favorite saying. I yelled out Marco and suddenly Melissa and I hear something yell Polo back. Celena on the other side heard nothing. It came from a small door that headed out on to the roof. I played back the audio and sure enough there was a voice saying Polo. Well it was getting late and that was the last thing we heard plus we had lots of video footage to go over so we headed back down to main floor to get ready to leave but before we left the ghost's had one more surprise in mind. Melissa couldn't leave because both of her headlights were burned out and it was dark outside. Maybe they wanted her forever to stay at the Winery. I love the winery and the owners and have enjoyed many years of investigations there. The wine tastes great too.

Listening for noises in the cellar

CHAPTER 14

OLD LICKING COUNTY JAIL NEWARK, OHIO

By Craig Nehring

Licking County Jail

This was a fun trip for many reasons. One of the places that we booked to stay while investigating here a place that looked like a garage that had a golf cart that came with it that we could cruise on around the campground. Rather than renting a hotel we decided to do something different. We were looking forward to this jail because Zak from Ghost Adventures was here and wanted to see what we could capture as well. So, on this adventures trip was Brandon, John, Rick, and me.

The History of Licking County Jail

In 1889, Old Licking County Jail was erected. The structure, with an almost castle-like appearance, was the creation of Joseph Warren Yost, an architect in the state of Ohio. Yost is well known for Ohio State University's Orton Hall. In its early days, many people believed that the jail was the sturdiest jail ever built in the state due to the use of Millersburg brownstone. The sandstone was quarried in Millersburg, Ohio and transported to the site.

The Old Licking County Jail was designed to serve two purposes. The front of the building had three levels. The first two levels served as housing for the Sheriff and his family. The first floor contained rooms, such as the kitchen, living room, office, and foyer. The second floor had bedrooms. On the third floor were the living quarters for the Jail's Matron. The back portion of the building served as the area in which the prisoners were incarcerated. The jail housed both male and female criminals in the thirty-two cells on separate floors. In total the Old Licking County Jail had the capacity to hold sixty-eight prisoners in the cells. Throughout the history of the jail the number of those incarcerated surpassed the max capacity of sixty-eight. Female prisoners were moved to another location during the 1970s. As of 1987 the incarceration of prisoners in the old jail ceased.

As many would suspect during the decades that the jail housed prisoners' countless tragic events occurred. There were several murders, suicides, and other deaths ruled as accidental, which took place. One of the most tragic events that took place during the jail's history involved Carl Etherington. Etherington arrived in Newark, Ohio in 1910. It was his job to locate saloons and speakeasies serving illegal alcohol and raid them. During one of those raids William Howard, a saloon owner, was shot and killed by Etherington. Angry over the murder of William Howard a lynch mob went to jail. The managed to break into the jail, locate Etherington, and then beat him with a hammer. If that was not enough, they took him outside and strung him up, hanging him from a telephone pole. It took the actions of Judson Harmon, governor at the time, to restore order. Also, four different sheriffs had heart attacks.

In 1987, a new jail was built, and the Old Licking County Jail's doors were officially closed.

The haunting of the jail was investigated by the show Ghost Adventures and many have come from all over to get a chance to investigate a place that was featured on TV. Teams that come investigate it have heard voices and seen dark shadows in the halls that disappear faster than they appear. Heavy footsteps can be heard on some of the floors above but when you go up there nothing is seen.

The Investigation of Old Licking County Jail

Our team at the time came down for two nights to investigate. We needed somewhere to stay so we picked this campground close by, but we decided to do something a little different and rent the garage out which was made into a handyman's dream. It had black and white checkered floor and bunk beds and of course a kitchen and shower. It came with a custom orange golf cart however it wasn't extremely fast, and the place overlooked a steam and large field nestled among the campers in the park.

We had everything ready to head out to the jail which was about a twenty-minute drive from us. As we approached the place looked massive from the outside and we had to wait a little while for our tour guide to get there so took the opportunity to take some pictures from the outside. The place reminded me of a castle all that was missing was the moat out front with the drawbridge. We saw a car pull in that had Ohio plates which makes sense since we were in Ohio, but John pointed out to me to look closer at the license plates on the car. The license plate said Spooked on it which is what my license plates say on my car from Wisconsin.

The side of the jail

Well the tour guide was ready to go so we headed inside to check it out. There were a couple levels of jail cells that were at the back of the jail with staircases. The front had some offices and where the sheriff and his family stayed. The first night we wanted to investigate in the cells, so we started out by sitting in some of the cells. The sun was just going down, and it was getting dark. I sat in one of the cells asking questions when suddenly it was like someone turned on a giant spotlight. The whole jail just lit up like daylight. Rick looked at John who looked at me. We walked to the windows to see all the lights around the jail were on. How are we supposed to investigate it looks like it's daytime and seeing shadows would be next to impossible? We headed down to talk to the tour guide to see what happened and why all the lights were on. She explained they had just installed those lights yesterday around the jail because there was some shady activity going on around town and break-ins. I thought wow great the day before we get there. We took a little break outside to gather our thoughts so we could figure how to go about our investigation. When she said things were shady, she wasn't kidding, and it seemed when it got dark the oddballs were out in this town. We noticed a drug deal go down in the alley with a couple people selling stuff out of their trunk we stayed away as we don't want to become casualties of the town. They walked toward me and said nice night for a ghost hunt and asked if we seen anything. I said, "Nope nothing at all yet."

I said let's try the darker areas down lower to see what we can hear in there and see if maybe the front sections are a little darker. The areas were a little darker in the office areas and some of the hallways away from the window. Brandon headed down toward the hallways by the cells with John while Rick and I investigated the offices area. We were walking up one of the staircases in the office area that leads to more offices and as we got to the top I clearly heard something walking up the stairs behind me and I asked if anyone was behind me. There was a loud thud on the stairs, but nothing could be seen. We were not in the darkened area of the offices and we were certain something was there with us and it was watching us. It seemed heavy in the room and Rick noticed it too. The feeling went away as quickly as it started, and all seemed quiet again. We headed back down to see how Brandon and John were doing in the hallways and found them sitting in the far corner of the hallway in whatever darkened area they could find. John said they were hearing banging on the cells and thought they saw some shadows. We stayed with them for a bit and heard a few bangs and what sounded like footsteps a floor above. We headed up there to check it out and sat in some of the cells. It was quiet again. I thought I heard voices and it sounded like children but know of no ghostly children reported. I still heard the voices however they were faint. I walked over to the wall and noticed one of the windows were open and I saw kids down on the street on some bicycles. I could hear them plain as day talking now about how the jail was supposedly haunted. I moved to one side of the window and in a low bellow said "Booo" only a nice long one. They looked up and started screaming and jumped on their bicycles and headed out of sight quickly. Rick and everyone were laughing about us becoming the ghosts. It was about midnight but figured we would try the cells on some of the other floors a little while longer plus we had one more night left anyways so leaving a little early to get some sleep would not be a bad thing.

The hallway between the outer wall and cells

Day two of our investigation and I also had a great idea to try to do a reenactment of a shooting. I picked up a cap gun at the store so I could pretend I was a prison guard going after a bad guy at the jail. I started in the cell area of the jail with my cap gun and I said that the prisoners were bad and anyone that tried to escape would be shot. Brandon played the prisoner and jumped out of his cell and I fired a couple shots off in his direction. Rick and John both thought they saw a shadow dart in my direction or at least out of the cell area. I said let's play back the audio and see what we hear. I played it back and right when I shot Brandon there was a voice saying, "I didn't do it and that hurts." Was that really a prisoner that thought we were shooting at them? We stayed in that area for a while longer and noticed some shadow play although it was hard with the streetlights outside again. It got quiet again almost as if the ghostly inmates were sleeping. We needed to take a break as it was quite warm inside, and the outside air was what we needed. We sat on the front porch for a bit. Brandon was standing down by the sidewalk by the road where there was more of a breeze, so I headed down his way. From the side of the building in the alley walked a girl maybe late 20s in very scantily dressed attire with fishnet stockings on. I looked at Brandon and he kind of grinned at me. She walked over to a car across the street got inside and well we all figured out what was happening after the second guy hopped in the car and out and that went on a couple times that night. Ironically, that was about the extent of the activity the rest of the night at the jail. It was an interesting jail and think it could be better without the streetlights. If the lights would be off, I would go back again.

Pictured are Rick, Craig, John, Brandon, and Jessica

CHAPTER 15

SHEBOYGAN INSANE ASYLUM
SHEBOYGAN FALLS, WISCONSIN
By Melissa Clevenger

Sheboygan Insane Asylum

My entire life has revolved around the paranormal, so it was no surprise when I moved to Sheboygan in 2001, that the Sheboygan

Insane Asylum would instantly pique my interest. Throughout the years living here I would hear stories about the old asylum just outside of town. Travis and I would always talk about how amazing it would be to someday investigate that place.

One day Travis was talking to Craig about the asylum and he told him that the asylum was the number one place that he would love to investigate. I could not agree more, but we knew that the building closed in 2002 and it was next to impossible to be invited inside. I will not get into all the details, but here we are today, the only team allowed to give tours of the Sheboygan Insane Asylum on a weekly basis.

As we continue to give tours to the public, we ask you, are you brave enough to venture these halls? Over 375,000 feet of darkness makes every investigation different. Seventeen wings span over four floors including underground tunnels where few have gone before.

To date as a team, we have spent well over 250 hours in the asylum investigating. The experiences and stories that we have witnessed inside those walls have been truly remarkable. From our first EVP in the building, to the first time the morgue was opened in over twenty years. We as a team continue to learn more about the Sheboygan Insane Asylum and the ghosts who inhibit the building.

The History of The Sheboygan Insane Asylum

In 1876, the Sheboygan County Asylum for the Insane was completed. The asylum began with eight patients that were being kept at the County Jail due to there being no suitable place to house them. Not long after opening it housed forty patients. Then on February 19, 1878, a fire broke out at the facility killing four of the patients. Of the four patients who passed away, one was listed as Billy Doe, an idiot, whose name was unknown.

Rebuilding of the asylum began almost immediately. The building was completed and fully furnished on June 1, 1882. As the years passed on, the need for more land to house the growing number of patients was imminent. Larger sections of land were purchased so that the asylum could continue to grow.

In 1938, the asylum was relocated to land about three miles from Sheboygan Falls. The new location could sustain 350 people and included a working farm that would become known as the poor farm. The building consisted of Y shaped wings with men on the North side and women on the South. Nurses would be housed onsite due to the rural location of the asylum. There was a separate boiler house and underground tunnels were used to enclose pipes and wiring.

On April 14, 1940, the new Sheboygan County Insane Asylum opened its doors. Glazed tile walls were used throughout the building so the staff could hose down the walls and floors for easy cleaning. Several years later a Library, Barber Shop, Beauty Shop, Fashion Boutique, and a Chapel were added to the building.

Forty-three German Prisoners of War were housed to work at the asylum in 1945. By 1963, the asylum had about 295 patients that included mentally deficient, mentally ill, and the mentally infirmed. From 1969 until 1978, the facility offered drug and alcohol rehabilitation.

In 1978, the mentally ill services were discontinued, and it became a county home for the developmentally disabled and chronically ill. By December of 2002, the building shut its doors and was put up for sale.

The Investigations of the Sheboygan Insane Asylum

It was a beautiful warm August day as Craig, Travis, and I drove out to meet the owner of the Sheboygan Insane Asylum for our first tour of the building. As we walked toward the front entrance of the building, I could only envision what we would see inside. I imagined instantly feeling all the energy in the building from all the souls inside; however, I felt nothing but excitement that we were actually here. We completed our full tour along with history and stories from the past. After this we began to plan our weekly Friday and Saturday night investigations that would be taking place here.

The stories that follow are just a few of the most memorable or to some the scariest nights that we have encountered at the Sheboygan Insane Asylum. Many of these stories happened while our team was giving tours to the public. We tell people that every night in the asylum is different, but the atmosphere and feel of the building often changes by the hour, so we never really know what the night may bring.

It was finally time for our team to investigate the asylum. We decided to begin on the second floor, which in the early days was the mentally challenged ward.

Instantly we began to hear loud bangs coming from the end of the wing. As the bangs continued Travis walked to the end of the wing to investigate, suddenly they stopped, complete silence. As he headed back toward the group at the beginning of the wing, the bangs started up again. Bang after bang, it got to the point that the bangs were coming on queue when we would ask.

The wing where we heard bangs and footsteps

As I played back my audio, I could clearly hear a child yelling. As loud as the sound of the child yelling was on my audio, I was surprised that we did not hear it with our own ears. The highlight of our first investigation at the asylum was when Craig had his ghost box on and said "Marco," and without skipping a beat, "Polo" was clearly said back to us. Craig is known for saying Marco Polo all the time, rarely do we get the response back of "Polo." After the ghost responded with "Polo" we could help but to start cheering with excitement.

On a very cold Saturday night I was investigating with Savannah and our friends from Minnesota, Heather and Kristen along with other guests. We began our investigation in the underground tunnels because it was still light outside and we enjoy investigating in the dark.

Kristen sat at the opening of one side of the tunnel, while Heather sat on the other end. It was not exceptionally long before the motion lights that we had placed far down in the tunnels began to turn on. This meant that something came close to the lights. Only seconds later our REM Pod began to go off. We sat there intently watching down the long tunnel when Savannah and Heather both noticed something coming toward Kristin. It seems like every time we see something in the tunnels everybody always starts to feel a cold draft, and this was no exception. Instantly my hands and face became ice cold as a chill came over me.

Savannah, Heather, Kirstin, Melissa

One night, Travis and I were investigating with a group in the left wing of the first floor. We were hearing the usual bangs and knocks coming from different rooms in the wing. I usually tell guests to sit in front of the doorways of each room because oftentimes people get touched by doing this. As one girl sat in front of one of the open doorways she suddenly jumped in the air and squealed because something had tapped her on her shoulder. After that everyone in the group could hear knocking coming from inside that room.

After a little while one of the guests who had an empty chair next to her asked if anyone wanted to sit by her. At that very moment, Travis heard clearly in his ear someone whisper "Yes." I was sitting right next to Travis and I had not heard a thing. Nobody believed Travis that he had just heard someone say "Yes." I decided to play back my audio to prove to him that nobody had said "Yes" to her question. Upon playback when she asked if anyone wanted to sit by her, there most defiantly was the answer "Yes." The voice was rather creepy sounding and instantly gave us the chills.

We have found that with each investigation we do at the asylum, for the most part, we hear the same names repeatedly. Often, the names we hear are only said on certain floors, which makes me wonder if they stay on the floors that they used to be on. Helen is one of the names that we hear all the time. She enjoys saying hi to us and telling us her name.

One day while we were in the rec area by the Chapel in the basement, we noticed a growth chart on one of the beams. To our amazement, we realized that five names on the growth chart were the exact names that we had been hearing on the ghost box every night. Helen was listed on the growth chart two times. Along with Tim, Joe, Jim, and Jeff, which were also names that come across the ghost box almost every night. This was incredible for us to see, and it gave us verification to what we had been there.

By now we have gotten to know the building and its occupants very well. The energy in the air has changed since our first visit here.

I can feel the spirits around us, and they now want their presence to be known. The building had never been investigated before our team came in, and I think that the ghosts are happy to finally have someone hear them and see them.

On one particularly cold night, Savannah and I headed down to the underground tunnels. As our group set up their chairs for our investigation, I pulled out the ghost box. Our session began with me asking who we were speaking to. The response we received was "I am Pete." I instantly asked Pete what he was doing in the tunnels with us, to which he responded, "That is a good question." Pete however never did answer us as to why he was in the tunnels, maybe he really did not know why he was there.

The tunnels in the asylum

We began to hear noises coming from the far-left side of the tunnel. In the depths of the darkness we could see a dark shadow creeping toward us. Just as soon as we saw the shadow it quickly disappeared from our view. Then the REM Pod began to go off and a cold draft swept past all of us.

This was not scary at all, what was scary was what happened next. Now we were all sitting there silently staring down the tunnel. Suddenly we noticed a ball of light coming toward us. We sat there in awe watching the ball of light move up and down coming closer and closer to us. Before I knew it, the ball of light came directly between Savannah and I, swooped down and moved upward as the size of the light grew.

I think everyone realized at the same time what was following the ball of light. Directly behind the ball of light, following its every move, was a bat! Panic set in with me immediately as I practically flew into Savannah's lap and tried to hide my head under her sweatshirt. I no longer was interested in the ball of light, I just wanted to get out of that tunnel.

We now decided to investigate in the living quarters where the original caretakers used to live. The living quarters are still set up with furniture from the 1940s. As we sat in the complete darkness several of us noticed that we could hear somebody whistling from down the hallway. The whistling began to sound eerie as it continued. We were almost in a trance listening to the whistling when our equipment began to go off startling us back to reality.

When we give investigation/tours of the asylum we always tell guests that every investigation is different. It is amazing how different every night is in the building. We have nights where activity in the building is constant and then hours later the building can be silent.

On an active night, we headed to the second floor to begin our investigation. As we began to ask questions and talk to the ghosts, I noticed that I could hear several people having a conversation to the left of me toward the other wing. Before I had the chance to say anything about what I heard, Travis announced that he heard people talking. About three people in our group had heard the conversation that was going on. We could not decipher what the spirits were talking about, but we do know that we heard it loud and clear.

Kara then saw something go directly in front of her face as she felt a force push her. She continued to feel something touching her arm when suddenly we all noticed a shadow peek out of one of the rooms three doors away from us. The shadow person seemed to be the height of a tall man. The shadow snuck its head back into the room and as soon as we stopped talking about it, it slowly began to peek its head out at us again. The night continued with the sounds of footsteps and knocks and sightings of various shadows.

Another active area that we enjoy investigating is in the boiler room. We all congregated into a large circle toward the back of the room. On either side of us were a set of stairs. On one set of stairs I sat my Mel Meter with REM and on the other set of stairs we sat Craig's REM Pod. We started with the ghost box to which we were getting highly intelligent answers to our questions.

Throughout our time sitting there, the REM Pods would go off on both sides of us. As the lights were flashing on our equipment telling us that something that we could not see was close by, we began to hear loud bangs coming from the top of the stairs. The bangs and knocks continued as we sat there, and they seemed to come closer to our group.

My stories of the asylum would not be complete without telling a few of the funny moments that we as a team have shared here. We take our investigating serious, but we have also learned that some of the best evidence that we get is sometimes when we are just hanging out and being ourselves. I am sure that the ghosts in the asylum have had plenty of laughs over our visits.

One night we were investigating in the surgical ward and we decided to all go into one of the surgery rooms to investigate. We sat there patiently asking questions and nothing was happening. Savannah then asked, "What are you doing in here?" To which I responded to her question with "We just wanted to try out one of the rooms to investigate instead of the hallway." She looked at me puzzled and then said, "I was talking to the ghost!" It was not the only time that night that I answered her questions to the ghost, I guess I was tired that night.

On another night we were investigating in the tunnels with the ghost box. Craig asked what the ghost were doing in the tunnels. To our surprise we received the response of "Drinking." Travis then asked what they were drinking, and we got the answer "Hennessy." Each night that we went into the tunnels we made it a point to ask these questions, and the ghosts always respond to us with "Drinking." However, each night they tell us that they are drinking a different type of alcohol. I like to think that the ghosts in the tunnel are enjoying us down there, and that they like to joke with us too.

As we wait for our investigations to start up again in the weeks to come, I often wonder if the spirits of the asylum are as excited as we are, waiting for our return. Are they patiently waiting for our team's arrival to the building? This really is one of my favorite places to investigate and the building and history is incredible. In the meantime, we are counting down the days until we can investigate the Sheboygan Insane Asylum again.

Through these halls we have shared laughs, we have shared screams, and ultimately, we have shared memories. Every investigation we do, brings us closer as a team. We seek answers to the unknown, we educate people on what we know, and to some people, we give hope. As we walk the long halls of the asylum, we can only begin to learn the stories of the past and continue to walk toward our futures.

Savannah, Melissa, Travis, Craig, Lloyd, Kara

The Rest of the Asylum Stories by Craig Nehring

The side view of a section of the asylum

Sometimes it all about the people you know to gain access to a site where no was has been able to go before. I heard the asylum was off limits to anyone that wanted to go there. All the teams that have tried to get in there and failed or went in there without permission and got arrested. I never go anywhere without getting proper permission. Travis and Melissa said no one can get access to this place and I like to always try my best to do so. Thanks to my team for getting me information to contact the owner. I gave him my ideas and asked if I could meet with him. He said we usually don't allow anyone in here at all and thanked me for my time and my ideas, but his stance was no. He said let me take your name down first in case I ever change my mind. After I said my last name he asked if I was related to John Nehring who owns the Grocery stores Sendiks and Groppi's in Milwaukee. I said he was my brother and he said those stores are well known and I used to go there all the time. He said come on down and we can talk and well here we are today doing tours at the Asylum.

When I got my first view and tour of the asylum, I was excited to go somewhere very few have gone before. I walked into the front entrance where they are working on the floor and peeling the old paint up to show the flooring from the 50s. They are working to restore the asylum and even making the front entrance into a coffee show sometime in the future. Inside that main there were doors leading into the wings of the building and before those doors was the original check in station with a glass window. I could imagine all the people checking in their loved ones and having to leave them there to get help. There was another staircase that went down to a lower level under the floor of that main room which was creepy on its own. The stairs from there went up to all the other floors as well and into the living quarters where the family that ran the hospital used to live. There was a couple bedrooms and a sundeck and kitchen that was all being remodeled as well. Once you walked out of that area you were on the second floor and there are seventeen wings and we had access to fifteen of them. All the wings looked almost the same and the patient's rooms were on both sides. There was also the area the nurses stayed in with a separate door leading up a few stairs with bedrooms and their bathrooms right off the bedroom. This was the only place in the building where the paint was peeling bad. This is also the place I was told that seven nurses or so had committed suicide. The third floor had the surgical center and offices and a bed pan dumper. Yes, I just said bed pan dumper where all the bed pans would be placed to dump, and I assume dumped into a holding tank in the basement. There were old hospital beds in there and dentist equipment from the dental room. There was a dark room for going over X-rays and film. I saw a buzzer that was a code red should anyone need help. I pulled it down and it worked lights flashed and a loud alarm was heard. There was rooftop access off the top of the elevator shaft that I got to walk out on, but our tours would not incorporate this for safety reasons. The elevator went down to the basement but there was something neat about the elevator when it was in the basement and that was the only place where the doors in the back of the elevator opened. That back area where it opened was the morgue and the very last tour, we had in 2019 guests got to see the morgue for the very first time in over twenty years.

The basement is an amazing place going in the form of a T. One hallway goes to the right and has a room with a chapel in it and the other side of the hallway goes to a breakroom with stuff still hanging from when the employees worked there. There was what looked like a little classroom for maybe some hands-on training. The other direction there was a bunch or different rooms including a laundry room and different stores like a library, Mexican food store, beauty parlor, and others for the patients to visit while there. The long part of the basement went into a very large section which was like an auditorium or meeting center where events had taken place and past that down a long hallway were coolers and then finally the tunnels that ran underneath part of the asylum and back to the boiler room.

Once outside on the property there were swing sets in the back yard and other buildings that had various uses. The huge water tower still stands on the property with rumors someone jumped to their death but was nothing I could confirm. The owner has a barn that people rent out today for weddings and other functions. There are goats that sound like they say your name when you walk close to them. I was frightened when I thought they said my name, but the owner said if you listen closely it sounds like they said his name too. The owner had two dogs and he said they bark at things that are not there and won't go inside the building for some reason. Might be the ghosts? There is no trespassing on the property here and those that do will be arrested and charged. There are cameras there that show the minute someone comes onto the property and the police are alerted.

The Best Times at the Asylum

Some reason I always get picked on by the ghosts in the asylum for instance once while investigating early in the beginning. I was in the chapel area known for negative activity even though you would think it should be peaceful. We had guests there that night and I was sitting on a chair and had the REM Pod behind my chair. We all heard a noise and the REM Pod lit up like crazy to tell us something was close by. Suddenly I felt a burning sensation on my back, and I lifted my shirt there were two scratch marks on my skin, and they were bright red. They didn't last long as they normally don't, and we didn't find out till later when Melissa went over audio that a ghost said, "That one." I assume they picked me when they said it. I got out of my chair and moved over to the other side and stood against the wall. I pulled the ghost box out to talk to them and through the box something said "Evil" and "Demon." Why would they be saying this in a chapel. We have been investigated places before to have some malevolent things in other churches as well so I shouldn't have been surprised almost like they were mocking religion. I stood there for a little bit and long enough for them to attack me again only this time it felt like they punched me in the back, and I was in some pain. I again I checked my back and it was bright red but without the scratches. I had just put my shirt down when a guest said they felt a cold draft shoot past them and another guest saw dark shadows move past them and out the door into the main area just outside of the room. I walked toward the door along with one guest and we both heard a sinister voice come from within the darkness. It sounded like it was laugh but was hard to make out and it wasn't a nice laugh but again like mocking. Many of our investigations of the chapel with guests had ended with guests feeling uneasy or sick feelings and some had to leave that area.

One night while in the boiler room, we were sitting in the back of the room asking questions in the dark when there was a loud pounding on something metal in the room. We searched for what it could be but found nothing. We also saw a figure of a man walk over toward the large boiler where they would clean out the bottom of the units. He disappeared faster then he appeared. We also found a metal rod moving back and forth and no one had touched it. Many of the guests have heard whispered voices come from the boiler room area. There is a staircase in the boiler room that leads to a bathroom that guests use and a couple guests have said the bathroom light has gone off while they were in there. They also claim that they hear noise while in there. I have yet to hear anything or have the light turn off on me.

One night while investigating one of the wings we had some amazing activity watching shadows peek in and out of the rooms. We all heard a loud dragging noise like something was being dragged across the floor and like always there was nothing. We also heard a little girl humming in the hallway, and I had walked in the direction of the humming after it had stopped and got to the very end of the hallway. I thought I heard a noise down by the stairwell and I asked if anyone were down there and to see if they could come my direction. I always say be careful what you wish for because something moved from the staircase right toward me, one loud footstep after another till it stopped right in front of me. I felt very uneasy and headed back toward the guests. One guest asked if he could walk down there and check it out, so he walked down where I was standing, and he heard a voice, and something move, and he didn't stay down there long either.

The boiler room area of the asylum

Another night I heard the same girl humming and we decided to play some music that night on our phone to see if anything respond. It seemed to wake up the place and maybe it's been a long time since they heard music. Now they wanted to dance in the hallways, and you could head bangs and knocks. I decided to take my SLS camera down there and check it out. The SLS camera picks up stick figures while using a series of green dots and is the same as using a Xbox Connect camera for gamers. I got about half way down when my camera picked up a figure standing right in front of me and I asked the figure to put out its right hand and amazingly it did and we caught it on the camera. I walked back to the guests and sat in my chair still pointing the camera down the hallway, but the figure was no longer there. I turned the ghost box on, and it said a girl's name Amy. I didn't ask if there was anyone named Amy there at all and I still had the SLS camera on and was scanning the guests and I could see that the figure was now sitting on one of the guest's laps. I told her the figure was on her lap and she said she felt something sitting there and her legs seemed warm. I asked here what her name was, and she said Amy. It was the same name the ghost said on the ghost box. The figure stayed for a way then left the area and all was quiet again.

While I can't tell all the stories that best one is the last tour of 2019 when for the first time in twenty years, we had the morgue open and it might have been a mistake. That night all hell would break loose and we had guests there as well. The morgue is so small that you can't even get five people in there side by side. Its not a big room but whatever was in there we let out. We started out the tour like every other tour and passed the morgue for people to look in and take some pictures. We then headed up to one of the wings and started out there. I of course again was picked on when something dug its nails into my back and my leg. I walked over to the other group, so I didn't alarm my group just yet. The other group was already getting activity and one of the girls on that group was scratched and wanted to see my scratches. There were raised red marks and burned and so did hers. She said let's go down to the main area and put something on there so I had one of the other investigators take over for me so we could take care of us. While we were putting lotion on another guest came down to where we were at and was holding his eye. Something punched him in the eye, and it was all swollen up. He was ok and continued the tour that night. We headed back up to the rest of the guests as we were doing better as well and hoping nothing else would happen and it didn't up in the wings. All was quiet now, so our next stop was down by the tunnels and the coolers in the basement and we had to pass the morgue again too.

Now down in the basement I decided to try sitting in the coolers with my group. The employees would say that when they went to get things out of the coolers that the door would slam shut on them even though it was wedged open. I had everyone sit in there and we asked some question, but it was quiet, and nothing slammed the door on us. I figured the next stop would be the tunnels and we can sit in there. We all lined up the chairs in the tunnel and started asking questions when we all got hit with this huge draft of air. It was so intense that it's like someone turned on a giant fan only super cold. At that moment, a guest saw a shadow block out the light at the other end and loud footsteps started coming our way till it the sound of them was right on top of us. One of the guests quickly turned on the lights and the shadow evaporated into the light and was gone. From behind us was a loud growl and with that one girl got sick and had to leave although she claims it was something, she ate prior to coming here. We headed back up stairs to help her out to her car where she is waiting for the rest of her group which still had two hours left. Well that was a remarkably interesting night and the last night we investigated there in 2019. I guess we will see what happens the first night of our new tours in 2020.

Investigating the tunnels in asylum

Getting ready for tours

CHAPTER 16

MINERAL SPRINGS HOTEL
ALTON, ILLINOIS

By Melissa Clevenger

Mineral Springs Hotel

Alton, Illinois has become one of my favorite towns to go on a girl's trip with Savannah on. The history of the town of Alton is amazing and it is no wonder that it is known as such a haunted town. Our trip consisted of four action packed days, just us girls.

Our agenda included going to a weekend conference, investigating the McPeak Mansion and finally investigating the Mineral Springs Hotel. Our first night in Alton we decided to drive around the town. At some point we ended up on a dark road on the west side of town that had fencing on the sides of the road. I instantly began to feel uneasy, but I couldn't describe why. Savannah began to complain about the same feelings that I was experiencing. We both felt uncomfortable and found it difficult to breath. There really is something about the land in Alton, you can just feel the energy in the air.

Finally, the time came for our investigation of the Mineral Springs Hotel. This would be the second time for Savannah and me to investigate the hotel. On our last trip we promised the owner that we would bring him some fresh cheese curds from Wisconsin so that would be our first stop once we were in the building. We both knew that this was going to be a great weekend.

The History of The Mineral Springs Hotel

Alton, Illinois has been said to be "one of the most haunted small towns in America." Throughout the town are numerous known haunted locations, among them in the downtown area is the former Mineral Springs Hotel.

The hotel was originally a meat packing company in the 1880s. The original plan by August and Herman Luer was to open an ice-making and cold storage facility. During the process of drilling for the well, it was discovered that a natural spring ran under the ground. The water from the spring had a strong smell because it was high in sulfur content. There were rumors that the water had healing therapeutic abilities. At this point the focus of the building changed.

In 1914, the Mineral Springs Hotel opened and was known as the most remarkable hotel in the Riverbend Region. The lowest sub-basement was located about five levels below the street, and this was where they started a water bottling plant. The hotel was built right above the water bottling plant. Upon opening the hotel became an immediate success.

In the lower levels they opened two mineral pools. One of the mineral pools was used strictly for men, while the other pool was open to all guests. Water from the spring was pumped directly into the pool. Guests believed that the mineral water in the pools had healing powers which made the hotel very well known.

As for the bottling plant, the hotel was selling over hundred bottles of water every day. They claimed that the natural spring water could heal everything from headaches to alcoholism. The hotel continued to thrive, and in 1926, August Luer sold the hotel. By the 1960s the hotel slowly began to deteriorate. Today it is known as the Mineral Springs Mall which features a few stores and is being brought back to its original glory.

There are several stories as to why the hotel may be haunted, although some of the stories have vary on the way they are told. One of the popular stories that is told is of an Italian artist who was staying at the hotel in the 1930s. The artist was unable to pay his hotel bill, so he agreed to paint a mural in the bar area to relinquish his bill. Before the mural was completed, the artist died never to complete his painting. Guests of the building often say that they smell cigar smoke, which could possibly be that of the Italian artists who stays at the hotel to this day.

One of the most popular stories at the hotel is that of the well-known Jasmine Lady. Upon staying at the hotel, the "Jasmine Lady" met another man and began to have an affair. Her husband caught them, and it is not known if she fell down the stairs or if her husband pushed her down. On several occasions guests of the building catch the smell of Jasmine perfume around the area of the stairs along with sightings of her.

There are also stories of people who had drowned in the large mineral swimming pool. One story is of a young girl named Cassandra who drowned in the pool, however there is no documentation of this happening. There is documentation about a man named Clarence who did drown in the pool which makes the pool one of the hot spots for investigating.

The investigation of the Mineral Springs Hotel

Our favorite spot to investigate inside the hotel is the large pool area, so we chose to save the best for last. Savannah and I met up with some of friends to investigate with and we all headed to the top floor. This floor is pretty much gutted out, but it does have a few hot spots that are good for investigating.

We began in a room that is rumored to have had a lady that hung herself in the closet, and she still hangs out around the room. We tried several attempts with the ghost box with no activity. Unfortunately, we were able to hear people at a nearby bar across the street. At one point I knocked on the wall and asked if anyone could knock back for us. Within seconds everyone in the room heard two loud knocks followed by what sounded like a voice. I decided to walk into what would have been the closet area for a little bit to investigate. I really did not have any activity in the closet, but I could feel a little differ-ent energy in that area.

Next, we were going to check out the smaller of the two pools which was known as the men's pool. Before we walked down the flights of stairs, I began to tell some stories of paranormal activity that was happening at my house. My son Kaleb is always talking about a boy named Darren who he says lives in our house. We took a little break in the hallway while I began to tell the stories of Darren.

I started with a story about when my son told me that Darren was standing next to me in the doorway. As I was talking, I noticed that the K2 Meter started to go off as well as the REM Pod that was a little bit away from us. We all stood there for a little bit and both pieces of equipment stopped going off. Then I finished my first story and both pieces of equipment went off.

My next story was about my son telling me that Darren was swinging on the swing at our neighbor's house across the street. When my son told me this he was just sitting there playing with his toys and he never looked outside. As I walked to the door to look at the neighbor's swing set, sure enough one swing was swinging high in the air as the other two swings sat perfectly still.

With every story that I told, each time that I mentioned Darren's name both the K2 and the REM Pod would go off. We began to test the equipment, and we talked about other non-related stories. Through all the stories the equipment sat quiet. I then decided to tell another story about Darren and instantly both pieces of equipment began to go off. I really am not sure if Darren is a spirit that follows me around or if he just came there when he heard me say his name, but I do know that he was there with us that night at the Mineral Springs Hotel.

After our little break we began to head down the stairs to the lower level men's pool. We had to walk down wooden beams to get into the pool which made it rather hard. Most of the time that we spent in the empty pool we laughed about how us girls had snuck into the all boy's pool. After about thirty minutes we had only heard a few noises, so we decided to move on to the big main pool.

The pool area is set up with chairs and a few trigger objects such as marbles and toys. Savannah and I decided to take some seats inside the pool along with the trigger objects. I began to roll some of the marbles down to the other end of the pool, mainly because there was not much else to do, when suddenly one of the marbles I rolled bounced back at us in the air. This happened a few times during our stay in the pool.

One of the investigators in our group noticed a black shadow move quickly at the other end of the pool. He pulled out his infrared camera and caught an image of a man standing at the end of the pool. He continued to follow the form on his camera as it moved closer to us. After a few moments he decided to shine his flashlight on the being only to discover that no one was there. Once he used his flashlight, he never spotted the black shadow again that night.

Our night was just about over all though we were really enjoying our time. We began to pack up all our gear and head back upstairs to our basecamp where we were keeping all our other equipment. The rest of this story will have to be continued because this is the perfect spot to talk about some of the dangers of ghost hunting.

Paranormal investigating is a true passion for me. I love the adventures that we get to go on, and I have been to so many amazing places through our travels as a team. Through these travels I have come to learn some of the many dangers that can be involved with ghost hunting.

My first danger to talk about is also my biggest fear. I am terrified of bats and they seem to be in a lot of the places that we investigate. At one location, Craig, Kara, and I were sitting around a table getting ready to be filmed for a new television show when all of a sudden, a bat came flying right by our heads and it kept swooping back and forth. I bet you thought the bat was the danger that I was going to write about. Nope, in a moment of panic over the bat I began to punch Craig in the arm repeatedly because I was so scared, and I didn't know what to do. I am sure that Craig walked away from that interview with several bruises on his arm.

Another danger of ghost hunting is that we investigate many places that are very dusty or even moldy. At one location the dust had me instantly coughing and my chest began to hurt. One other location that we investigated had recently been flooded and you could see the water lines on the walls, and I could smell the mold in the air. After both locations I was rather sick for a few weeks following.

My final three stories about some of the dangers of ghost hunting all occurred on the trip that Savannah and I took to Alton, Illinois. As a team we travel not only throughout Wisconsin, but to several known haunted locations throughout the United States. On the way to Alton, Savannah and I came up to a van that was fully engulphed in flames. As we got closer to the vehicle it began to have several small explosions. No, our vehicle did not catch on fire, but through our travels we have seen so many accidents and we know that there is always a chance that something can happen while we are traveling.

Van that was on fire on our trip

Flooding over the roads

As we got closer to Alton, Savannah and I did not completely know what to expect. The entire town of Alton had been flooded by the Mississippi River for several weeks. We had looked forward to our trip for so long that we were unwilling to give it up, even though we knew there was a chance that the flooding could get worse while we were there. Upon arriving in Alton, many of the main roads had been shut down and the water was right up to all the buildings.

When ghost hunting always be mindful of your surroundings, safety is always our number one concern. My final story of some of the dangers of ghost hunting is something that I would have never thought would be a problem, and it is the continuation of my original story at the Mineral Springs Hotel.

As we headed up the stairs to our basecamp room it was about 2 a.m. and by this time we were all exhausted. Savannah got in the room first and she sat down on a bench that had a cushion on it. I decided that the spot right next to her seemed like a good seat, so I plopped right down next to her. Pain instantly shot up through my butt and after a few moments of shock I realized I had sat directly on a needle. I quickly flew up, only to discover an exceptionally large old rusty needle sticking straight up from the cushion. The needle was sticking up so perfectly that it almost seemed as if someone had planted it there.

Unfortunately for me, I was very overdue for a tetanus shot and I am extremely afraid of needles. Our investigation ended with me having to go to Urgent Care to get a tetanus shot. I was having bad pains toward the back of my knee and the doctor said that was caused because the needle I sat on must have went through a nerve. Weeks later I was advised that I would need to be tested for other things that may have been on that rusty needle. My new saying is that "Ghost hunting can be a real pain in the butt."

In the end we encountered what could have been a lot of dangers on our trip to Alton. Would I go back next year and do it all again, absolutely. Savannah and I look forward to our trip to Alton all year long. There are so many haunted locations throughout the town and so much history. The Riverbend Region is well worth the drive to investigate.

Rusty needle I sat on

Savannah and Melissa in Alton

CHAPTER 17

THE HOMESTEAD
WISCONSIN RAPIDS, WISCONSIN

By Craig Nehring

The Homestead

I happened to know Wayne that lets teams do overnights at this place. He is friends with the owner of First Ward in Wisconsin Rapids as well, so getting in here to investigate was easy. We will get the history out of the way first before getting into the investigation.

The History of the Homestead

Built in 1897 by Authur Haferman. They rasied cattle, pigs, chickens, and had croplands. Arthur died in the house as well as another person and their funerals were actually held inside the house. There seems to more ghosts there then just them which brings me to another thing I like to tell people that ghosts do not have to die in a place to make it haunted. Ghosts can come and go as they please. So if there is more than one ghost in the house and its not related to anything that happened in the house it might be ghosts that are just passing through or found the place to be somewhere they wanted to visit or maybe even that they know someone.

The Investigation of the Homestead

I arrived on site first of course not before grabbing a bite to eat and waiting for Sheila to get there to eat too. She arrived and I handed her some food I picked up for her and we were standing in what I will call a breezeway just inside the entrance of the house. Off that breezway was the basement. Sheila was just standing in there when she said that her leg burned. We looked at it and sure enough there was a small scratch that went away quickly. Some will say to us oh that's demonic and no that is not the case and very rarely do you find demonic hauntings. The normal ghost can scratch you as well. We stood there for a few minutes more talking to something that we heard moving in the basment. Something was down there and maybe it was the something that just scratched her. We were about to head to the living room when she now was getting pinched by something on her butt. It must be a male ghost because I am having nothing happen to me just her. I said lets take a tour of the house and get you away from the basement.

The tour of the house started in the breezway and headed up a few steps to the kitchen. The otherside of the kitchen had the livingroom with a couch to sit on and off the living room was a staircase that went to the second floor. The second floor had all hardwood floors. There were a few bedrooms and a bathroom. Off the second floor was another staircase that went up to the attic. I was told the second floor and the attic were hot spots for paranormal. Our last stop of the tour was down in the basement and it was an old basement some concrete but mostly dirt floors and it still needed to be cleaned some as past people that lived there left stuff scattered. There was a canning room with tons of jars of food the problem was it was outdated by yeers and I am not sure how many years but there were green beans that looked like ghost green beans. They were white with mold and many other vegtables that looked so bad that if one fell off the shelve it might kill you. We left the basement to head back up and wait for one last investigator named Jodi who was coming from Green Bay.

Well Jodi made it and it was dark now so time to investigate. We headed to the basement first to ask some questions there. Sheila was a little worried that something would pick on her again in that area. We stood down in the dark and asked some questions to who was there. Something moved on the far end of the basement and stopped a couple feet away from us and the air got ice cold. I played back the voice recorder to see if anything answered us and I caught someone saying that they were not down in the basement. I think they were lying since we heard them moving around and also making the air ice cold. Whatever was there was not bothering Sheila now it was keeping it's distance but still making noises like moving things but we couldn't see them move or find what was moved. There were a couple loud bangs but it finally went quiet. We decided to head upstairs and sit on the couch and be really quiet to see if we could hear anything come from within the house like footsteps or whatnot. It was kinda cold so and there was no heat in the house so I had a blacket and we were sharing that. Sunddenly, there was loud crash that came from the top of the stairs followed by footsteps that ran up to what sounded like the attic. Another loud thud was heard and the thud was so intense that we swear some of the loose paint on the ceiling came down. Well we know where we were going next. We headed upstairs and into the attic. It was actually quiet up there not too much moving around at all and even asking questions didn't turn up any results. I said maybe we should go down to the bottom of the attic on the second floor and just sit in the hallway. I had Sheila sit all the way down on one end and Jodi near the attic and I was in the middle. We were asking some questions and I had the REM Pod sitting halfway up on the stairs to the attic. I said something like why are you making all that noise. Well they decided to make more noise just then and stomped hard on the attic floor but then came down the stairs one by one a loud thud. Jodi had no part of that she jumped up away from the entrance to the attic and ran past me jumping over my legs in the process and stopped down by Sheila at the other end since we always say saftey in numbers. Well the ghost stopped at bottom of attic and my flashlight revealed nothing of course like always. I asked again if something was there. There was and it moved past me and I felt the cold breeze as it passed me in the hall. It made it to the girls where it also became ice cold. They moved away from that side of the hallway to see if it wanted to go into one of the rooms. A door next to them slammed shut and we all jumped. There was now something in the room or it wanted the door closed and was still in the hallway with us.

The stairs leading to second floor

I walked over to the closed door and opened it and peeked inside. Nothing was there it was empty and very quiet. The last thing we heard was what sounded like something running down the carpeted stairs to the first floor and then down another flight meaning its in the basment now.

Our last stop was the basement to see if it was down there. We stayed down there and it was getting much colder in the house not so much from cold spots but it was cold outside. It was really quiet even though we knew something was there it must have wanted to be left alone or it went to bed. We called it a night but we had fun and would like to return sometime in the future on a warmer evening.

CHAPTER 18

FARRAR HAUNTED SCHOOL MAXWELL, IOWA

By Melissa Clevenger

Farrar school

Although I had never heard of the Farrar Elementary School prior to our team planning a conference there, I was extremely excited to experience this haunted school for myself. I couldn't think of a better weekend, an old haunted school along with some amazing speakers.

Upon arrival to the school, I couldn't help but notice the old cemetery across the street. I was also surprised to see such a large school basically in the middle of nowhere. As we began to unload our equipment from the vehicle, I could not even think about ghost as the hot humid air stopped me in my tracks. Thankfully, the school had one room that had an air-conditioner running.

As we walked into the school, it really did have a creepy feeling to it. I could not wait to explore the school and investigate later that night. As other team members and guest began to arrive, our weekend was finally ready to begin.

The History of Farrar Elementary School

In the early 1900s there were several one room schoolhouses located throughout the countryside in rural Iowa. In 1919, a local farmer named C.G. Geddes donated 6 acres of his farmland so that a larger school could be built to merge all the one room schoolhouses together.

The new school opened its doors in 1922 and would be called Farrar Elementary School. At 17,000 square feet and a price of $100,000, the school was large for such a small town. Some local residence was not pleased claiming the school was to elaborate with its indoor restrooms, boiler heating, and electric lighting. On April 1, 1922, there was a commencement for the grand opening that included a banquette for hundreds of citizens while an orchestra played on stage in the auditorium.

After eighty years of educating, the school closed its doors on May 3, 2002. Farrar school closed its doors the same way that it originally welcomed guests in as an orchestra played on stage in the auditorium once again. The schoolhouse sat vacant for another five years before it was purchased by the current owners in 2006.

It is not known why the Farrar school has become one of the most haunted schools in Iowa. There are no documented cases of deaths in the school history. Across the road from the school sits a cemetery that is 150 years old. The population of the small town is now only thirty people and the only population growing in the town is in the local cemetery. As the years go by, the stories of the haunted school in the middle of Iowa continue to be told. With each investigation, the investigators have new haunted stories of their own to add to the haunted history of Farrar.

The graveyard across the street

The Investigation of The Farrar Elementary School

As darkness began to fall on the sky, it was now time for us to investigate. We began our investigation in the boiler room which was directly off the gym area. Closing the door behind us closed off the outside world and brought us into complete darkness.

At this point we were only a small group investigating consisting of Craig, Kara, Savannah, a few guests, and myself. We decided to start with a ghost box session to try and talk to any ghosts that were in the building with us. Instantly we were receiving intelligent responses to our questions. The answers we were receiving were not what we expected though.

The entity talking to us had almost a demonic voice and was telling us that there was a portal in the room with us. We continued to talk to this entity until suddenly I caught what looked like a person standing in the doorway to the right of me. Before I could even say that I saw someone standing there, Kara exclaimed that she saw someone in the doorway. As the group of us continued to look at the figure in the doorway, Craig decided to shine his light toward that direction, and nothing was there.

Next a small group of us investigated in what used to be the principal's office. We were given the opportunity to test out some new equipment that some of our speakers for the event had brought. We were receiving some interesting answers and conversations, but the majority did not really make sense with what we were asking.

Another area that our team has had good experiences is in the Library. We each took a seat at a desk to begin our investigation. The room was incredibly quiet as we sat there in the dark. Before long, our REM Pod began to go off with each question that we asked. Savannah asked if she could read whoever was with us a story, and right away the REM Pod went off lighting up. So, we sat there in that room as Savannah read a story to us and whatever ghosts were in the room with us at that time.

I would say my favorite place to investigate in the Farrar Schoolhouse would be the auditorium. One thing that I have learned investigating is that sometimes you receive your best evidence when you are just being yourself. We must realize that the ghosts were once people to. If we are joking around and having fun, the ghosts sometimes like to join in.

I decided that since we were in a school and might possibly be dealing with the ghosts of children, we should play some games. As a group we sat in a large circle and proceeded to play duck-duck-goose.

Before we started the game, we asked who was with us and a girl that sounded like a child said her name was "Katie." The fun part of this game was that we left an empty spot for Katie to play along with us. We laughed so hard as we took turns running around the circle and of course letting Katie do the same.

Once we got tired of running around in circles, we decided to start a new game. This game we called "ball on ball," and it consisted of sitting in a circle and throwing a ball at the ball in the middle, in the hopes of it rolling to another player. We continued to play games; we were having so much fun that we were not even aware if anything paranormal was going on.

The auditorium

As we started to tire from our game, I noticed that one of the people in our group was staring intently at the auditorium doorway.

I quickly turned my head toward the doorway where I could clearly see a tall skinny man standing in the doorway watching us. I honestly could not tell if I was seeing someone standing there from our group or if I was staring at a ghost. I continued to watch the man in the doorway as the others carried on talking.

After staring intently at the man for a solid five minutes Kristin tapped me on the shoulder and said, "Do you see what I see?" I asked if she was referring to the man standing in the doorway to the left of us, to which she replied, "Yes!" We did not take our eyes off the man in the doorway as Craig shined his flashlight at him. As the light hit the man there was nobody there. I could not believe it; I had been staring at this man for countless minutes and just like that he vanished. I quickly jumped up to investigate the hallway to make sure nobody was there, but there was nothing.

It is very possible that maybe the old principle was just checking in on us to see what we were doing. I am not sure who was watching us as we played our games in our large circle. Interacting with the ghosts in this manner was such an enjoyable experience. We continued our night by investigating a few other locations throughout the school before we headed off to bed for the night.

During the early hours of the morning, Savannah and I headed toward the gym where the bathrooms were located. As Savannah was getting ready, I sat by the entrance of the bathroom and I could hear a few people talking in the gym and shuffling around. I continued to listen to the conversations in the gym, when I began to wonder who was out there. As I peered out the bathroom doorway, I soon realized that the gym was completely empty. There was not a soul around anywhere near that gym.

My team has investigated the Farrar School numerous times throughout the years. This was my first time there, and I am very amazed with the experiences that we had. I am ready for the next chance we get to go to that small town in the middle of nowhere to see what Farrar has in store for us on our next trip there.

Craig, Savannah, and Melissa in front of school

Kara, Savannah, Johnny, Melissa, Kirstin, Korin

Lockers that open and close on their own

Craig would like to thank Nancy and Jim Oliver for many years of investigations.

CHAPTER 19

DIVINE INTERVENTION
By Craig Nehring

Divine intervention, fate, or destiny happens every day and every hour all made up by choices. Some people say you choose your own fate or your destiny. Everytime you go somewhere you change your destiny sometimes good sometimes bad. If you were to take your dog for a walk and you walk him around the block the same way all the time but one time you decide to go left at the corner instead of right. In taking that right a car jumps a curb and kills you. Lets hope not but you take the risk of something different happening going a different way or even the same way. You decide one day to take a car ride somewhere but you have no specific place in mind to go so you just drive. When you come to the stopsign you have the choice to go many different ways but what way will you choose and each way you go has an outcome. One way might lead to a very scenic park and one way might go to a winding river. So all in all your destiny could be just around the corner.

Some of your friends are met this way. I once had my car in a car show in Elkhorn Wisconsin in the early 80s and I was into low riders back then. I saw these two lowered trucks there and walked over to talk to the owners. There was a guy there by the name of Chuck

Griffith who happened to know a girl that went to high school with me and we got to talking. I invited him up north to Minocqua where I lived to do some fishing. He came up for about a week to hang out and fish and many more times after that as well. We became close friends all by a chance meeting by going to a car show. Everything you do leads you to find new exciting places to explore or meet new people.

Ghost hunting is the same way. You choose to investigate a building trying to capture something amazing. Maybe it's a voice or footsteps but you need to be in the right place at the right time. So what direction will you go first? I like to go to the places in the building where the most activity is found and hope something comes out of that. It's all by chance and fate.

Some say they met their girlfriend or boyfriend under unique curcumstances. A friend of mine was stuck in a snowstorm and couldn't make it home from his hotel so he had to stay one night longer. He met his current girlfriend that night at the hotel bar because they were unable to leave due to bad roads. So was that fate or destiny or maybe even divine intervention.

Equipment Used On Investigations

REM POD

REM Pod uses a mini telescopic antenna to radiate its own independent magnetic field around the instrument. This EM field can be easily influenced by materials and objects that conduct electricity. Based on source proximity, strength, and EM field distortion four colorful LED lights can be activated in any order or combination. The REM Pod is intended to further help promote and advance paranormal research.

MEL METER

The **Mel Meter** is a dual-purpose combination unit that measures both EMF (electromagnetic field) and temperature simultaneously. The meter was designed and developed by Gary Galka of DAS Distribution Inc. Gary lost his oldest of three daughters, Melissa. After Melissa's passing, some incredible things started to happen. The meters model number denotes his daughter's year she was born and the year she died.

THERMAL CAMERAS

Ghosts are knowns for using the heat around them as energy, which ends up causing a fluctuation in the areas' temperature. Since thermal cameras can detect and show changes in temperature, an unexplainable cold or hot spot could mean there is a ghost present. By using these devices, ghost hunters can take a better glimpse into the realm of the paranormal.

It is usually assumed that ghosts dwell within the colder levels of the spectrum, however, that is not always the case. Therefore, it is so important to investigate all abnormalities in the area and not just cold spots. Paranormal activity will usually not be seen by the human eye, and display on the screen as either a dark or bright spot. Warm spots will usually be brighter, and cold ones darker.

EDI

EDI is the meter for ghost hunting and paranormal investigations with so much more to offer.

- EMF change detection
- Temperature change alert
- Digital temperature readout
- Geophone vibration detection

SLS CAMERA

This camera will detect humans and animals in absolute darkness or full light. It also seems to see bodies when there is nothing there the naked eye can see, spirits? It works much like the SLS camera at a fraction of the cost! You can record video directly to the tablet or to SD card.

Here's how it works: It uses an RGB camera with depth sensor and infrared light projector with a monochrome CMOS sensor which sees everything not as a flat image, but as dots arranged in a 3D environment. These 1000s of infrared dots allow the camera to "see" depth and detail like a sonar. The installed software can recognize people by distinguishing body parts, joints and movements. If shows a person shaped object on the screen that you cannot see with the naked eye then there is something there the IR is detecting and the programing is recognized as a human shape based on body parts and joints together.

BOO BEAR

Boo asks EVP questions in order to trigger a response. If anything changes (EMF, motion, temperature) Boo will respond appropriately, letting us know that we may not be alone. Set Boo down and turn it on to detect environment changes and start asking questions. Make sure to set a recorder or camcorder near the doll to document any potential responses. Children will love it, but this is not a toy. When it comes to ghost hunting and paranormal investigations, some theories suggest that using an object familiar and attractive to an entity may entice them to interact.

DVR SYSTEM
DVR systems with night vision can be a powerful way to capture great paranormal evidence. Using multiple cameras, you can record and cover large areas for long periods of time with one easy setup.

GHOST BOX
Ghost boxes and spirit boxes and a great way to promote communication in both directions with a potentially intelligent entity. A ghost box utilizes various environmental queues through software to give the spirits a voice while a spirit box emits raw radio frequencies.

GHOST GRID
High-powered laser emits a grid of green dots useful for detecting shadows or general visual disturbances during an investigation. Set it in front of a running camera to catch potential evidence. You can adjust the size and shape of the stars by turning the adjustable lens. Detach the lens and it will function as a high-powered laser pointer.

LINKS
Fox Valley Ghost Hunters – Facebook
fvghosthunters.com

ALSO AVAILABLE FROM LULU.COM VOL 1